Acknowledgements

We would like to acknowledge the following individuals for their input during the development of the series:

Salam Affouneh
Higher Colleges of Technology
Abu Dhabi, U.A.E.

Kristin Bouton
Intensive English Institute
Illinois, U.S.A.

Nicole H. Carrasquel
Center for Multilingual Multicultural Studies
Florida, U.S.A.

Elaine Cockerham
Higher College of Technology
Muscat, Oman

Danielle Dilkes
CultureWorks English as a Second Language Inc.
Ontario, Canada

Susan Donaldson
Tacoma Community College
Washington, U.S.A

Penelope Doyle
Higher Colleges of Technology
Dubai, U.A.E.

Edward Roland Gray
Yonsei University
Seoul, South Korea

Melanie Golbert
Higher Colleges of Technology
Abu Dhabi, U.A.E.

Elise Harbin
Alabama Language Institute
Alabama, U.S.A.

Bill Hodges
University of Guelph
Ontario, Canada

David Daniel Howard
National Chiayi University
Chiayi

Leander Hughes
Saitama Daigaku
Saitama, Japan

James Ishler
Higher Colleges of Technology
Fujairah, U.A.E.

John Iveson
Sheridan College
Ontario, Canada

Alan Lanes
Higher Colleges of Technology
Dubai, U.A.E.

Corinne Marshall
Fanshawe College
Ontario, Canada

Christine Matta
College of DuPage
Illinois, U.S.A.

Beth Montag
University at Kearney
Nebraska, U.S.A.

Kevin Mueller
Tokyo International University
Saitama, Japan

Tracy Anne Munteanu
Higher Colleges of Technology
Fujairah, U.A.E.

Eileen O'Brien
Khalifa University of Science, Technology, and Research
Sharjah, U.A.E.

Jangyo Parsons
Kookmin University
Seoul, South Korea

John P. Racine
Dokkyo Daigaku
Soka City, Japan

Scott Rousseau
American University of Sharjah
Sharjah, U.A.E.

Jane Ryther
American River College
California, U.S.A

Kate Tindle
Zayed University
Dubai, U.A.E.

Melody Traylor
Higher Colleges of Technology
Fujairah, U.A.E.

John Vogels
Higher Colleges of Technology
Dubai, U.A.E.

Kelly Wharton
Fanshawe College
Ontario, Canada

Contents

The Inside Track
to Academic Success

Student Books

   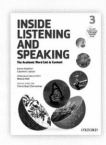 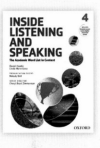

For additional student resources, visit: www.insidelisteningandspeaking.com.

iTools for all levels

The *Inside Listening and Speaking* iTools component is for use with a projector or interactive whiteboard.

Resources for whole-class presentation

> **Book-on-screen** focuses class on teaching points and facilitates classroom management.

> **Audio and video** at point of use facilitates engaging, dynamic lessons.

Resources for assessment and preparation

> Customizable Unit, Mid-term, and Final Tests evaluate student progress.

> Complete Answer Keys are provided.

For additional instructor resources, visit:
www.oup.com/elt/teacher/insidelisteningandspeaking.

About *Inside Listening and Speaking*

Unit features

> **Explicit skills instruction** prepares students for academic listening

> **Authentic videos** from a variety of academic contexts engage and motivate students

> **Pronunciation instruction** ensures students are articulate, clear speakers

ARCHITECTURE

UNIT 1

Recycled Buildings

In this unit, you will
> learn about recycled building materials.
> increase your understanding of the target academic words for this unit.

LISTENING AND SPEAKING SKILLS
> Using Abbreviations in Notes
> Signal Phrases in a Speech
> **PRONUNCIATION** Noun Phrases

Identifying the unit's goals focuses students on the **listening and speaking skills** and the academic topic.

Self-Assessment
Think about how well you know each target word, and check (✓) the appropriate column. I have...

TARGET WORDS	never seen this word before.	heard or seen the word but am not sure what it means.	heard or seen the word and understand what it means.	used the word confidently in *either* speaking or writing.
AWL				
assemble				
♪ assume				
bulk				
♪ component				
♪ construct				
contrary				
♪ element				
extract				
♪ factor				
innovate				

Self-assessment prepares students for the vocabulary in the audio and video activities.

The Academic Word List and the Oxford 3000

Based on a corpus of 4.3 million words, the **Academic Word List (AWL)** is the most principled and widely accepted list of academic words. Compiled by Averil Coxhead in 2000, it was informed by academic materials across the academic disciplines.

The **Oxford 3000™** have been carefully selected by a group of language experts and experienced teachers as the most important and useful words to learn in English. The Oxford 3000 are based on the American English section of the Oxford English Corpus.

Oxford 3000 and Academic Word List vocabulary is integrated throughout the unit and practiced in context through audio and video resources.

Explicit Skills Instruction

About the Topic

Architects do more than design how buildings will look. They also choose the materials that the building will be made of. In this guest lecture, you'll learn about using unusual materials to build environmentally friendly homes.

Before You Listen

Read these questions. Discuss your answers in a small group.

1. Would you ever like to build your own home? Why or why not?
2. What materials (wood, bricks, etc.) are buildings on your campus made from?
3. Have you ever made something new out of old materials? Explain.

Listen

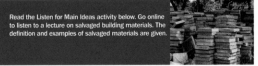

Read the Listen for Main Ideas activity below. Go online to listen to a lecture on salvaged building materials. The definition and examples of salvaged materials are given.

Listen for Main Ideas

Mark each sentence as *T* (true) or *F* (false). Work with a partner. Restate false sentences to make them correct.

___T__ 1. Re-using materials is the best way to make a "green" building.

_____ 2. Salvaged materials are some of the most expensive resources to use.

_____ 3. A converted bus can have running water and electricity.

_____ 4. George Sorvino found car parts on the Internet.

PRESENTATION SKILL   Signal Phrases in a Speech

LEARN

Signal phrases are words or short phrases that help you organize a speech or a presentation. They introduce ideas and examples. They are also used to identify key ideas. Signal phrases help your listeners understand your ideas and how they connect.

Introducing an idea	Giving examples
I'm going to talk about …	For example,
The topic of today's presentation is …	… such as …
We'll begin with …	In this case,

Connecting ideas	Summarizing
First, / Second, / Third,	In summary,
Next, I'd like to talk about …	To summarize,
Finally,	To sum up,

A. Read the lists of signal phrases with a partner. Think of other signal phrases you may have heard. Add them to the lists.

B. In the audio clip, the lecturer says: "Good afternoon. Today I'm going to talk to you about some really creative sustainable homes." What kind of signal phrase does she use here?

C. Look at the following sentences from the audio. Underline the signal phrases. Discuss with your partner what those phrases signal.

"I'll begin today's talk with a brief overview of using salvaged materials in architecture. Then, we'll discuss two very interesting ways that ordinary people

---

Discussion questions activate students' knowledge and prepare them to listen.

Comprehension activities help students understand the listening materials in preparation for academic skills instruction.

Listening and speaking skill instruction is linked to the academic content. **Apply** sections give students the opportunity to practice the skills in context.

High-Interest Media Content

Before You Watch

Read these questions. Discuss your answers in a small group.

1. How can recycling and reusing materials help us to minimize the effects we have on the land and water around us?
2. People often say a home's value is "all about location, location, location." What do you think this saying means?
3. Would you live in a building made out of recycled materials? Why or why not?

Watch

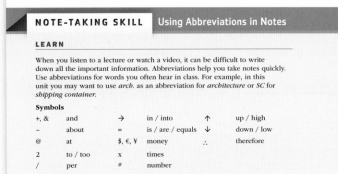

Read the Listen for Main Ideas activity below. Go online to watch a video about "green" architecture. A lecturer gives some background information on this architectural trend, then shows a video clip of one example.

> **Audio and video** including lectures, professional presentations, classroom discussions, and student presentations expose students to a **variety of academic contexts**.

> **High-interest, original academic video** and authentic BBC content motivate students.

Listen for Main Ideas

Mark each sentence as *T* (true) or *F* (false). Work with a partner. Restate false sentences to make them correct.

_F_ 1. Ian Felton's apartment surprises his friends because it is next to a river. *His home surprises his friends because it's made of shipping containers.*

___ 2. Apartment buildings can be made out of recycled shipping containers.

___ 3. Shipping containers are primarily used to send goods from Europe and North America to Asia.

___ 4. Shipping containers are an inexpensive kind of building material.

___ 5. Ian Felton's apartment building is the only one of its kind.

NOTE-TAKING SKILL   Using Abbreviations in Notes

LEARN

When you listen to a lecture or watch a video, it can be difficult to write down all the important information. Abbreviations help you take notes quickly. Use abbreviations for words you often hear in class. For example, in this unit you may want to use *arch.* as an abbreviation for *architecture* or *SC* for *shipping container*.

Symbols

+, &	and	→	in / into	↑	up / high
~	about	=	is / are / equals	↓	down / low
@	at	$, €, ¥	money	∴	therefore
2	to / too	x	times		
/	per	#	number		

Pronunciation Instruction

PRONUNCIATION SKILL — Contrasting Old and New Information

LEARN

In spoken English, you use stress to highlight important *focus words*. A focus word is the main, or most important, idea in a sentence. Focus words may also signal a new topic. Effective speakers get the listener's attention by stressing focus words.

A. Go online to listen to the words and phrases below. Notice the focus words (in pink) in each phrase.

Stress Pattern	●●●	●●	●●●	●●●●●
Word	commission	diverse	prohibit	congratulations
Phrase	I'm finished.	With what?	my project	It took forever.

B. Go online to listen to the following dialogue. You may hear several stressed words. Notice how old, repeated information is unstressed because it is no longer new or important. This creates a strong contrast between the focus word and the rest of the words in the sentence.

A: Yay! I'm finally finished!

B: Finished with what?

A: My final project. It took forever!

B: Congratulations! You deserve a break.

A: I need a break. And I need to get out of here.

B: Let's go to a movie.

A: We pretty much always go to the movies.

B: Then how 'bout a café?

A: I usually study in a café. That's where I do all of my work. Plus I've been doing a lot of sitting.

B: We could go for a walk downtown …

A: It's usually pretty crowded there at this time of night. What about a walk around the lake? We could take in the lights.

B: I'll get my jacket!

C. Go online to listen. You will hear the stressed syllable of the focus word, then the focus word, and finally a complete sentence from the dialogue in activity B. Listen and repeat.

Example:

fi / finished / I'm finally finished!

Recycled Buildings

In this unit, you will
> learn about recycled building materials.
> increase your understanding of the target academic words for this unit.

LISTENING AND SPEAKING SKILLS
> Using Abbreviations in Notes
> Signal Phrases in a Speech
> **PRONUNCIATION** Noun Phrases

Self-Assessment
Think about how well you know each target word, and check (✓) the appropriate column. I have...

TARGET WORDS	never seen this word before.	heard or seen the word but am not sure what it means.	heard or seen the word and understand what it means.	used the word confidently in *either* speaking or writing.
AWL				
assemble				
🔑 assume				
bulk				
🔑 component				
🔑 construct				
contrary				
🔑 element				
extract				
🔑 factor				
innovate				
minimize				
sustain				
🔑 transform				
utilize				

🔑 Oxford 3000™ keywords

Vocabulary Activities

Sustain means "to make something continue for a long period of time" or "to provide enough to keep someone or something alive and healthy."

*Celia has **sustained** her high grades by visiting the tutoring center every day.*

*Generous portions of fruits and vegetables **sustained** the children.*

The adjective *sustainable* means "involving the use of natural products and energy in a way that does not harm the environment" or "that can continue or be continued for a long time."

*Using old building materials is a **sustainable** way to create new buildings.*

CORPUS

A. Work with a partner. Discuss the sources of energy in the box. Decide whether each source is *sustainable* or *unsustainable*.

batteries	natural gas	solar power	wind power
coal	oil	tidal power	wood

Sustainable	Unsustainable
wind power	

B. People often ask for advice. However, one piece of advice can be contrary to another. With a partner, match the advice from the first column with contrary advice from the second column.

*"Forget about the past" is **contrary** to "Learn from previous mistakes."*

____ 1. Enjoy the moment.   a. Always plan for tomorrow.

_d_ 2. Forget about the past.   b. Respect only those who respect you.

____ 3. Respect everyone you meet.   c. Follow other people's examples.

____ 4. Always be yourself.   d. Learn from previous mistakes.

Word Form Chart		
Noun	**Verb**	**Adjective**
assumption	assume	assumed
construction	construct	constructive
innovation innovator	innovate	innovative
_____	minimize	_____
transformation	transform	_____

C. Using the target words in the Word Form Chart, complete the paragraph below. Be sure to use the correct form and tense of each word. Use the words in parentheses to help you.

In the 1800s, Henry Bessemer created a new, _innovative_ process for
(1. original)

making steel. Steel was expensive compared to other kinds of metal used

in _____ at the time. But steel is a much stronger and safer building
(2. building things)

material. Utilizing the Bessemer process _____ the cost of making
(3. reduced)

steel. This _____ how factories and buildings were designed and built.
(4. changed)

Steel may always be needed for some buildings. But more and more people

are interested in "green" architecture. Its use of building materials is

_____ architecture again. Architects _____ that "green," or
(5. altering)   (6. believe)

sustainable, materials will become more popular over the next decade.

D. What tools do people utilize in each of the following professions? Share your answers with a partner.

1. firefighter
   hose, axe, fire truck, and helmet
2. scientist
3. football player

4. mechanic
5. author
6. fashion designer

About the Topic

Green architecture is building design that uses environmentally friendly methods and materials. Environmentally friendly materials either use less new material, can be used again, or are re-purposed from another use. What are some environment-friendly materials you've heard of for building houses?

Before You Watch

Read these questions. Discuss your answers in a small group.

1. How can recycling and reusing materials help us to minimize the effects we have on the land and water around us?

2. People often say a home's value is "all about location, location, location." What do you think this saying means?

3. Would you live in a building made out of recycled materials? Why or why not?

Watch

Read the Listen for Main Ideas activity below. Go online to watch a video about "green" architecture. A lecturer gives some background information on this architectural trend, then shows a video clip of one example.

Listen for Main Ideas

Mark each sentence as *T* (true) or *F* (false). Work with a partner. Restate false sentences to make them correct.

_F_ 1. Ian Felton's apartment surprises his friends because it is next to a river. *His home surprises his friends because it's made of shipping containers.*

___ 2. Apartment buildings can be made out of recycled shipping containers.

___ 3. Shipping containers are primarily used to send goods from Europe and North America to Asia.

___ 4. Shipping containers are an inexpensive kind of building material.

___ 5. Ian Felton's apartment building is the only one of its kind.

NOTE-TAKING SKILL   Using Abbreviations in Notes

LEARN

When you listen to a lecture or watch a video, it can be difficult to write down all the important information. Abbreviations help you take notes quickly. Use abbreviations for words you often hear in class. For example, in this unit you may want to use *arch.* as an abbreviation for *architecture* or *SC* for *shipping container.*

Symbols

+, &	and	→	in / into	↑	up / high
~	about	=	is / are / equals	↓	down / low
@	at	$, €, ¥	money	∴	therefore
2	to / too	x	times		
/	per	#	number		

Words

A	answer	des	design	Q	question
aka	also known as	esp	especially	re:	about
b/c	because	Ex	example	sm	small
betw	between	imp	important	u	you
bldg	building	lg	large	w/	with

A. Read the lists of abbreviations with a partner. Which abbreviations do you already use? Which ones are new to you? Add two to three more abbreviations to each list.

B. Read the following sentence from the video. Compare the full sentence to the abbreviated notes.

"Next we're going to watch a video clip about an **innovative** movement in green architecture, also known as **sustainable** architecture."

Video innovative movemt in gr. arch, aka sustainable arch

APPLY

A. Circle the abbreviations in the sentences. Then write out the complete sentence.

1. ②　advan of SCs = strength & cost.

   Two advantages of shipping containers are strength and cost.

2. It's imp 2 des homes u will want 2 spend time in.

   _____

3. SC homes = a good choice 4 ppl who want 2 b green.

   _____

B. Watch the first part of the video. Use abbreviations to complete the notes below.

1. green arch. = pop. approach 2 _____*bldg des*_____

2. _____ = min. impact of new constr. on our envmnt.

3. Mats should b local, renewable, and _____

4. _____ focus of new model of _____

5. Des'rs and archs r transforming _____

C. Go online to watch the second part of the video again. Take notes. Use abbreviations.

1. When you finish, review your notes and and compare your abbreviations with a partner.

2. What were some common words you heard repeated during the video? What abbreviations did you use for those words?

3. Use your notes to retell key ideas from the video.

Vocabulary Activities

Assemble means "to come together or bring things or people together in a group" or "to fit all the separate parts of something together."

> The manager **assembled** the employees for a meeting.

> She took pieces from old bicycles and **assembled** a new bicycle.

Re-, meaning "again" and *dis-*, meaning "not" can be added to the front of *assemble* to create *reassemble* (*assemble* again) and *disassemble* (take apart).

> My desk fell apart, so I need to **reassemble** it.

> My car's engine was making strange noises, so I had to **disassemble** it and fix it.

CORPUS

A. Read each sentence. Work with a partner to decide if each is an example of *assemble*, *reassemble*, and / or *disassemble*. There may be more than one answer for each.

_____assemble_____ 1. I just bought a new desk, and I need to put it together.

_____ 2. Our bookcase fell apart, so I put it back together.

_____ 3. My family met at the park for a celebration.

_____ 4. The shed in our backyard is old, and I need to take it apart.

The noun *factor* means "one of the several things that influences a decision."

> Money was one **factor** in her decision to take a second job.

> Grades are one **factor** in deciding whether a student receives a scholarship.

CORPUS

B. Imagine you are deciding which university to attend. Rank these factors from most important to least important. Explain your reasons to a partner.

____ cost of tuition   ____ if friends attend there

____ located near family   ____ size of university

____ reputation of university ____ scholarship offered by university

Word Form Chart		
Noun	**Verb**	**Adjective**
bulk	_____	bulky
component	_____	component
element	_____	_____
extraction	extract	extracted
_____	minimize	minimized
sustainability	sustain	sustainable

C. Complete the paragraph below using the correct form of the words in the Word Form Chart. Use the words in parentheses to help you.

Although big houses are popular, some people have begun moving into "tiny houses." They're very small and often built with ___*sustainable*___ materials. But
(1. renewable)

what are the _____ of a tiny house? First, they are tiny! Most have
(2. features)

only 29 to 250 square feet of floor space. It's hard to fit a lot of _____
(3. large)

things in there! In fact, there is usually space for only the most basic items.

Second, vertical space is important. Tiny houses make use of floor-to-ceiling

storage spaces. The sleeping space is _____, so beds are often located
(4. made smaller)

near the ceiling. Third, tiny houses are usually built on trailers for easy

movement. You can _____ your house from an undesirable location if
(5. remove)

it's on wheels! Last, the _____ of everyday living, such as a shower or
(6. pieces)

stove, need to be tiny, too. People who want to live a simpler life with very

little "stuff" should look at a tiny house as a possible new home!

D. What do these people do with the bulk of their time? Complete the sentences. Compare answers with a partner.

1. A musician spends the bulk of her time ___*playing music*___.

2. Architects spend the bulk of their time _____.

3. Students spend the bulk of their time _____.

4. A mechanic spends the bulk of his time _____.

About the Topic

Architects do more than design how buildings will look. They also choose the materials that the building will be made of. In this guest lecture, you'll learn about using unusual materials to build environmentally friendly homes.

Before You Listen

Read these questions. Discuss your answers in a small group.

1. Would you ever like to build your own home? Why or why not?
2. What materials (wood, bricks, etc.) are buildings on your campus made from?
3. Have you ever made something new out of old materials? Explain.

Listen

Read the Listen for Main Ideas activity below. Go online to listen to a lecture on salvaged building materials. The definition and examples of salvaged materials are given.

Listen for Main Ideas

Mark each sentence as *T* (true) or *F* (false). Work with a partner. Restate false sentences to make them correct.

_T_ 1. Re-using materials is the best way to make a "green" building.

___ 2. Salvaged materials are some of the most expensive resources to use.

___ 3. A converted bus can have running water and electricity.

___ 4. George Sorvino found car parts on the Internet.

PRESENTATION SKILL   Signal Phrases in a Speech

LEARN

Signal phrases are words or short phrases that help you organize a speech or a presentation. They introduce ideas and examples. They are also used to identify key ideas. Signal phrases help your listeners understand your ideas and how they connect.

Introducing an idea	Giving examples
I'm going to talk about ...	For example,
The topic of today's presentation is ...	... such as ...
We'll begin with ...	In this case,

Connecting ideas	Summarizing
First, / Second, / Third,	In summary,
Next, I'd like to talk about ...	To summarize,
Finally,	To sum up,

A. Read the lists of signal phrases with a partner. Think of other signal phrases you may have heard. Add them to the lists.

B. In the audio clip, the lecturer says: "Good afternoon. Today I'm going to talk to you about some really creative sustainable homes." What kind of signal phrase does she use here?

C. Look at the following sentences from the audio. Underline the signal phrases. Discuss with your partner what those phrases signal.

"I'll begin today's talk with a brief overview of using salvaged materials in architecture. Then, we'll discuss two very interesting ways that ordinary people have turned salvaged structures and objects into homes. Finally, I'll read you a brief section of my book."

APPLY

A. Listen to the lecture again. Write down the signal phrases you hear. Compare your list in a small group, and add any you missed.

B. Work with your partner to organize your signal phrases into the categories. If some signal phrases from the lecture don't fit into the categories, describe new categories.

C. Discuss the following question with a partner. You will use this response to give a short speech using signal phrases.

Would you ever live in a home constructed of salvaged materials, such as shipping containers? Why or why not? Give three reasons.

D. Use your answer to activity C to create a short speech using signal phrases.

1. Begin with a signal phrase that introduces your opinion. For example, "In this speech, I will talk about ... ."
2. Use signal phrases to give examples and connect your ideas.
3. Summarize your opinion, using a signal phrase.
4. Practice your speech before presenting it to a small group.

PRONUNCIATION SKILL   Noun Phrases

LEARN

A *noun phrase* is a group of words centered around a noun. Two common examples are compound nouns (noun + noun) and adjective + noun descriptions. Two guidelines will help you to recognize and produce the correct stress patterns in noun phrases. Applying these rules will help you to express yourself clearly.

Guideline 1: Stress the first element	Guideline 2: Stress the second element	
Compound nouns	Descriptions	
noun + noun	adjective + noun	adjective + compound noun
1. a building component	5. recycled materials	9. recycled shipping containers
2. water conservation	6. renewable energy	10. old light bulbs
3. energy consumption	7. sustainable construction	11. green building materials
4. an apartment complex	8. an important factor	12. modern living spaces

A. Go online to listen to the compound nouns in 1–4. Stress the first noun that makes up each word.

B. Go online to listen to the adjective / noun phrases in 5–8. Stress the noun in each phrase.

C. Go online to listen to the adjective / compound noun phrases in 9–12. Stress the first element of the compound noun.

APPLY

A. Practice the noun phrases in the chart above with a partner.

B. Ask your partner to guess a compound noun from the chart in Learn. Listen to his / her answer and give feedback on the stress.

> A: You use these to light your house.   B: Light bulbs.
> A: Stress the first noun.   B: **Light** bulbs.
> A: Nicely done.

C. Discuss these questions in a small group. Include noun phrases from the chart in your answers. Pay close attention to the stress patterns.

1. How is your home energy efficient or not efficient?

2. How might you transform your current living situation into greener, more energy-efficient housing?

3. What are some other ways that you can minimize your impact on the environment?

End of Unit Task

In this unit, you learned how to use abbreviations in your notes and organize a speech with signal phrases. Review these skills as you listen again to the lecture on sustainable materials and prepare a speech. Use at least four of the unit vocabulary words in your speech.

A. Listen again to the lecture on sustainable materials (see p. 8). Use abbreviations to complete the notes below.

Bldg w/ salv. mat.

1) Popular b/c: 2) Problems
   a) Cheaper   a) more time
     - _____ % less $ b) more work
     Ex. Oak wood flr, new is 3x $ - esp. making mat. → right shape
   b) Easy 2 find   Ex. _____
     - @ arch. salv. yards
     - _____
     Ex. door knobs

3) Creative salv. bldgs
   a) Whole bldg from 1 thing
     - already shaped 2 fit people + things
     Exs. shipping container, _____
   b) Bldg made of many things
     Exs. Car parts: roofs, _____

B. Imagine that your city is going to build a new community center in your neighborhood. City planners ask for residents' opinions about the new building. You and your partner plan to give a speech asking them to be "green."

Use your completed notes from Presentation Skill Learn, activity A to plan your speech. Decide with your partner who will present each part.

Introducing an idea	Giving examples
I'm going to talk about …	For example,
The topic of today's presentation is …	… such as …
We'll begin with …	In this case,
Connecting ideas	**Summarizing**
First, / Second, / Third,	In summary,
Next, I'd like to talk about …	To summarize,
Finally,	To sum up,

C. Choose a signal phrase for introducing an idea, and write the first sentence of your speech.

_____

D. Divide your speech into three parts. For example, Partner A: three elements of green architecture and Partner B: three questions to ask before choosing materials. Write your three topics here. Choose signal phrases to connect your ideas.

1. _____
2. _____
3. _____

E. For each topic, give an example. Choose signal phrases from the list.

1. _____
2. _____
3. _____

F. Finish your speech with a signal phrase that summarizes your ideas. Write your conclusion.

_____

G. Practice your speech. You and your partner will practice your speech with another pair of students. Remember to use correct stress in noun phrases.

H. Give your speech to the class.

Self-Assessment		
Yes	**No**	
☐	☐	I successfully took notes using abbreviations.
☐	☐	I successfully used information from my notes to write a speech.
☐	☐	I introduced and summarized my speech using signal phrases.
☐	☐	I connected my ideas and gave examples using signal phrases.
☐	☐	I used appropriate stress in noun phrases.
☐	☐	I can correctly use the target vocabulary words from the unit.

Discussion Questions

With a partner or in a small group, discuss the following questions.

1. What are the principles behind green architecture?
2. Why is green architecture good for the environment?
3. Do you think it's more important for architecture to be "green" or beautiful?

Rethinking City Spaces

In this unit, you will

> learn how people are using design to keep cities healthy places to live.
> increase your understanding of the target academic words for this unit.

LISTENING AND SPEAKING SKILLS

> Using a T-Chart to Take Notes
> Supporting Your Opinion in a Discussion
> **PRONUNCIATION** Contrasting Old and New Information

Self-Assessment

Think about how well you know each target word, and check (✓) the appropriate column. I have...

TARGET WORDS	never seen this word before.	heard or seen the word but am not sure what it means.	heard or seen the word and understand what it means.	used the word confidently in *either* speaking or writing.
AWL				
🔑 capacity				
🔑 civil				
🔑 commission				
🔑 contrast				
🔑 criteria				
diverse				
enhance				
eventual				
🔑 inevitable				
🔑 invest				
isolate				
prohibit				
scheme				
🔑 significant				

🔑 Oxford 3000™ keywords

Vocabulary Activities

A. Read the sentences. What do the **bolded** words mean in the context of the sentence? Choose the correct definitions. Use a dictionary to help you.

1. The new museum has the **capacity** to hold 1,200 people.

   a. the number of things or people that a container or space can hold

   b. the ability to understand or do something

   c. the official position or function that somebody has

2. In **contrast** to predictions, the Olympic Games went quite smoothly.

   a. the fact of comparing two or more things in order to show the differences between them

   b. differences in color or in light and dark

   c. a person or thing that is clearly different from somebody / something else

3. We need to **isolate** the sick patients.

   a. separate a part of a situation, problem, idea, etc. so that you can see what it is and deal with it separately

   b. separate a single substance, cell, etc. from others so that you can study it

   c. separate somebody / something physically or socially from other people or things

4. The company decided to **diversify** its interests.

   a. change or make something change so that there is greater variety

   b. develop a wider range of products, interesting skills, etc. in order to be more successful or reduce risk

   c. increase in volume or get more

5. Many cities are learning to **invest** in better public spaces.

   a. spend money on something in order to make it better or more successful

   b. buy property, shares in a company, etc. in the hope of making a profit

   c. give somebody power or authority, especially as part of their job

6. The southwest region has developed a very successful irrigation **scheme**.

   a. a large-scale plan

   b. to make a plan about how to do or undertake something

   c. a plan to cheat people out of something

The adjective *inevitable* means "that you cannot avoid or prevent."

*It was **inevitable** that the rent would go up because it was so low at the start.*

We use the adverb *inevitably* to mean "as is certain to happen."

*We began the meeting about the problem project and **inevitably** ended up discussing it for hours.*

We use the noun *inevitability* to refer to something that we are unable to avoid or prevent.

*Paying taxes is one of the great **inevitabilities** in life.*

CORPUS

B. Identify the form of *inevitable* used in each sentence. Write *ADV* (adverb), *ADJ* (adjective), or *N* (noun) next to the sentence. Then work with a partner to restate each sentence using a different form of the word.

_N_ 1. The inevitability of a rainstorm every day is something you learn to live with in Singapore. *Rainstorms every day are inevitable in Singapore.*

___ 2. We inevitably felt bad about the loss because we had wanted so much to win.

___ 3. The loss of some sales in a down market is inevitable, but they should recover as the economy improves.

C. The word *civil* has several different meanings. Match the definitions on the left with the example sentences on the right.

_a_ 1. connected with the state government, and not connected with any other organization

a. I'd like to get a job in civil service.

___ 2. involving personal legal matters, and not criminal

b. I don't get along with my manager, but we are civil to each other.

___ 3. formal or polite, but not very friendly

c. Disagreements between neighbors are often handled in civil court.

D. A *commission* is a group of people in charge of studying an issue or problem. Complete these sentences with a form of *commission*.

1. A map of the area ___was commissioned___ in 1806 by Tyrion J. Weatherford.

2. The group studying the Green River wants to _____ a new bridge for pedestrians.

3. The project _____ was planning to decide who got the job, but they could not come to an agreement.

About the Topic

Many urban areas are rapidly growing so that several large cities become one large "concrete jungle." These huge urban areas are known as "megacities." This extreme urbanization creates concerns for city planners and residents. How can megacity residents get relief from city life or have a sense of community when they have millions of neighbors?

Before You Listen

Read these questions. Discuss your answers in a small group.

1. Where would you prefer to live: the city or the country? Why?

2. What places in a big city would you purposely go or avoid going?

3. Does the area where you live have a strong sense of community?

Listen

Read the Listen for Main Ideas activity below. Go online to listen to an interview about how one city planner feels we might improve life in megacities.

Listen for Main Ideas

Read the questions about the interview. Work with a partner to choose the best answer to complete each sentence.

1. According to the interview, the world's fast-paced urban growth is causing ___.

   a. the development of megacities

   b. a better sense of community

   c. a greater appreciation for high rises and larger structures

2. Urban planners of megacities want to encourage ___.

   a. people to move to the city and to live in high rises

   b. a sense of community and the incorporation of natural areas

   c. more subways and places such as restaurants and cafes

3. The city planner generally ___.

   a. is for the development of megacities

   b. wants to improve the living environment in large cities

   c. thinks designs using natural areas are too expensive

NOTE-TAKING SKILL Using a T-Chart to Take Notes

LEARN

You can use a T-chart during a lecture or presentation to quickly list information about two sides that are discussed. For example:

- Pros and cons
- Advantages and disadvantages
- Questions and answers
- Problems and solutions
- Facts and opinions

A T-chart will help you be able to examine both sides independently and together.

Pro	Con
Megacities offer a lot of interesting activities for residents.	There are often not a lot of parks in megacities.

Fact	Opinion
According to a recent survey, 25% of the residents feel the city doesn't have enough parks.	I think more parks are needed in this area.

APPLY

A. Listen to the first part of the interview again. Complete a T-chart with questions and answers that you hear. Then compare your chart with a partner. Did you note the same information?

Questions	Answers

B. Listen to the second part of the interview again. Complete a T-chart with facts and opinions that you hear. Then compare your chart with a partner. Did you note the same information?

Facts	Opinions

Vocabulary Activities

A. Each word in the box is a synonym for one of the target words below. Put each word from the box in the correct column. Use your dictionary as needed. Compare your results with a partner.

concluding	future	magnify	raise
final	improve	outlaw	resulting
forbid	increase	prevent	stop

enhance	eventual	prohibit
improve	_____	_____
_____	_____	_____
_____	_____	_____
_____	_____	_____

The adjective *significant* means "important" or "large enough to be noticed." The adverb form is *significantly*.

*Having children resulted in several **significant** changes in her lifestyle.*

*The same book was available at another store for a **significantly** lower price.*

The noun is *significance*, which means "the importance of someone or something."

*I never understood the **significance** of being a member of Phi Beta Kappa.*

 CORPUS

B. List three significant examples for each topic. Explain your list to a partner.

1. Challenges in your life:

   studying for tests, getting a driver's license, moving to a new country

2. Successes at school:

   _____

3. Differences between your life now and your life ten years ago:

   _____

4. Benefits from improving one's ability to speak English:

   _____

As a noun, *contrast* is "a difference between two or more people or things that you can see clearly when they are compared." It is often used with the prepositions *between*, *into*, *with*, *in*, or *of*.

*The **contrast** <u>between</u> the first and the second attempts were clear.*

*We did better with this year's sales <u>in</u> **contrast** <u>to</u> last year's.*

*Her green shirt **contrasted** nicely <u>with</u> her blue trousers.*

*The **contrast** <u>of</u> blue against white really made the image sharp.*

CORPUS

C. Work with a partner to complete the sentences with the correct prepositions.

1. She noted the contrast _____*in*_____ style between the first speaker and the second.

2. There was a lot of contrast _____ the two types of painters.

3. _____ contrast _____ previous years, the contestants were early this year.

Criteria is the plural noun form of *criterion*. A *criterion* is a standard a person uses when making a decision or forming an opinion.

*To graduate, students have to meet the following **criteria**: (1) maintain a 2.5 grade point average, (2) pass all classes their senior year, and (3) apply for graduation.*

*The most important **criterion** for finding a house is location, in my opinion.*

CORPUS

D. What criteria do these people or places need to meet in the following situations? Make a list. Discuss your answers in a small group.

1. applying for a job:

   have a college degree, have experience in the field, be able to speak English

2. getting a five-star rating as a hotel:

   _____

3. being the leader of a country:

   _____

E. Circle the best words in parentheses to complete the sentences. Use a dictionary to help you understand new words. Compare answers with a partner.

1. The city started a special (*capacity* / (*commission*) / *criteria* / *scheme*) made up of city council members to decide on the project.

2. Frankly, their business just doesn't have the (*capacity* / *commission* / *criteria* / *scheme*) to handle all the new orders.

3. There are several (*capacity* / *commission* / *criteria* / *scheme*) that you have to consider when changing jobs such as pay, opportunities, and location.

About the Topic

City planners often develop civil projects to improve a neighborhood. Occasionally, they ask for ideas from residents to give them an opportunity to become involved in city development. By allowing the people who live in an area to take part in planning for a city's future, everyone feels involved and shares in the success of the project.

Before You Watch

Read these questions. Discuss your answers in a small group.

1. Do you think cars should be kept out of certain parts of your city? Why or why not?

2. In what ways do parks benefit a community?

3. What are some places where younger people can hang out and enjoy themselves in a city or town?

Watch

Read the Listen for Main Ideas activity below. Go online to watch a classroom discussion. Listen to the students decide on the most important criterion for a project to improve their city square.

Listen for Main Ideas

Read the questions about the discussion. Work with a partner to ask and answer these questions.

1. Why is the class having the discussion?

2. What are the three projects the students discuss?

3. Which project do the students support in the end?

SPEAKING SKILL   Supporting Your Opinion in a Discussion

LEARN

During a class discussion, you often need to share your opinion. When possible, use facts to support your opinion. Supporting your opinion helps others to see your point of view. Look at the following example:

Opinion: I feel more comfortable walking near the river since the city added more lights.

Opinion supported by fact: I feel more comfortable walking near the river since the city added more lights. According to the paper, there are a lot more people walking there in the evenings as well.

You can use the following phrases when supporting your opinion in a discussion.

Supporting your opinion		
With examples	**With expert opinions**	**With data**
For example ...	According to ...	Data show that ...
Like ...	To quote ...	The numbers suggest that ...
Such as ...	The article / book states that ...	Research suggests that ...

APPLY

A. Read the expressions for supporting opinions below. Then watch the discussion again. Number the phrases in the order you hear them. Listen again. What does each expression refer to? Compare your answers with a partner.

____ I read an article where a researcher said ...

____ According to the guideline ...

____ For example ...

____ The journalist who wrote it argues that ...

____ ... such as ...

____ That survey by the mayor's office showed that ...

____ The chapter we read in our book last week said ...

B. Read the cues. Make statements as if you are supporting an opinion. Be sure to use the correct phrase for the correct type of information.

1. A time you couldn't drive in an area.

   For example, the streets were blocked in my city one time, and it was really frustrating to get around.

2. A magazine article stating, "45 percent of young people enjoy going to the park."

3. The mayor of your city claiming, "We need a really imaginative approach to our main square."

4. A suggestion for three good books to read in your local library.

5. A city council report saying, "Young people should have a place to go in the city."

6. Research that says, "Most people want parks."

C. Now discuss which of the following projects you would choose for your city center or one near you. Remember to support your opinions.

Project 1: Open a youth center with activities for young people.

Project 2: Commission a number of art works by a famous artist to be placed in the area.

Project 3: Feature a light show that plays on weekend nights to draw visitors.

LEARN

In spoken English, you use stress to highlight important *focus words*. A focus word is the main, or most important, idea in a sentence. Focus words may also signal a new topic. Effective speakers get the listener's attention by stressing focus words.

A. Go online to listen to the words and phrases below. Notice the focus words (in pink) in each phrase.

Stress Pattern	●●●	●●	●●●	●●●●●●
Word	commission	diverse	prohibit	congratulations
Phrase	I'm finished.	With what?	my project	It took forever.

B. Go online to listen to the following dialogue. You may hear several stressed words. Notice how old, repeated information is unstressed because it is no longer new or important. This creates a strong contrast between the focus word and the rest of the words in the sentence.

> A: Yay! I'm finally finished!
>
> B: Finished with what?
>
> A: My final project. It took forever!
>
> B: Congratulations! You deserve a break.
>
> A: I need a break. And I need to get out of here.
>
> B: Let's go to a movie.
>
> A: We pretty much always go to the movies.
>
> B: Then how 'bout a café?
>
> A: I usually study in a café. That's where I do all of my work. Plus I've been doing a lot of sitting.
>
> B: We could go for a walk downtown ...
>
> A: It's usually pretty crowded there at this time of night. What about a walk around the lake? We could take in the lights.
>
> B: I'll get my jacket!

C. Go online to listen. You will hear the stressed syllable of the focus word, then the focus word, and finally a complete sentence from the dialogue in activity B. Listen and repeat.

Example:

fi / finished / I'm finally finished!

A. Go online and listen to the dialogue again. Underline the one word in each sentence that gets your attention. (It is usually the last content word or a new piece of information.) Check your choices with a partner.

B. Circle the stressed syllable for each focus word in the dialogue on page 22. Practice the dialogue with a partner. Be dramatic. Exaggerate. Create contrast by making the focus words extra strong, extra long, and extra high. Clearly give less stress to other words in the sentence.

End of Unit Task

In this unit, you learned how to take notes using a T-chart to examine two sides that are discussed. You also learned how to support your opinion using examples, expert opinions, and data. Review these skills by first listening to a presentation and noting the main facts and opinions about the topic.

 A. Listen to a presentation about a city issue that must be resolved. Fill in the T-chart to note and identify the pros and the cons of the options discussed.

Pros	Cons
Option 1	Option 1
Option 2	Option 2
Option 3	Option 3

B. Review your notes and choose which project you think would be best for the city. Use a T-chart to list the reasons why and information you can give to support each reason.

Reasons	Supporting information

C. In a group, choose one project. Share your opinions with the group. Explain why you think the others should agree with you. Support your opinions with examples, expert opinions, and data from the T-chart you made in activity B.

D. Choose one person to share your group's decision with the class. Explain why you chose the project you did. As a class, vote for the best project for the city.

Self-Assessment		
Yes	**No**	
☐	☐	I successfully chose the best type of T-chart for each lecture.
☐	☐	I successfully made statements to support an opinion using new phrases for introducing examples, expert opinions, and data.
☐	☐	I successfully supported my opinions in a discussion.
☐	☐	I can use word stress to emphasize focus words.
☐	☐	I can correctly use the target vocabulary words from the unit.

Discussion Questions

With a partner or in a small group, discuss the following questions.

1. Which issues of urban planning do you think are most important?
   a. Making a city beautiful.
   b. Making a city environmentally friendly.
   c. Making it easy to travel within a city.
2. What public features do you think cities need to have to be good places to live?
3. Is it important to plan features for smaller towns?

High-Tech Art

In this unit, you will

> learn about three-dimensional (3-D) printers and digital art.

> increase your understanding of the target academic words for this unit.

LISTENING AND SPEAKING SKILLS

> Comparison and Contrast

> Summarizing Information

> **PRONUNCIATION** Chunking, Intonation, and Sentence Focus

Self-Assessment

Think about how well you know each target word, and check (✓) the appropriate column. I have…

TARGET WORDS	never seen this word before.	heard or seen the word but am not sure what it means.	heard or seen the word and understand what it means.	used the word confidently in *either* speaking or writing.
AWL				
abstract				
consent				
🔑 convert				
dynamic				
🔑 function				
identical				
🔑 instance				
🔑 layer				
mechanism				
🔑 period				
🔑 precise				
🔑 revolution				
🔑 technical				
virtual				

🔑 Oxford 3000™ keywords

Vocabulary Activities

Word Form Chart			
Noun	**Verb**	**Adjective**	**Adverb**
abstraction	abstract	abstract	abstractly
conversion	convert	converted	_____
function	function	functional	functionally
layer	layer	layered	_____
period	_____	periodic	periodically
revolution	revolutionize	revolutionary	_____
_____	_____	virtual	virtually

A. Complete the paragraphs about 3-D printers using the correct forms of the target words in the Word Form Chart.

As more people start to use them, 3-D printers are _revolutionizing_ the printing
(1. changing)

and business worlds. Inventors use 3-D printers to see if trial designs actually

_____ before producing them in large numbers. Architects use them
(2. perform well)

to _____ 2-D plans into 3-D models to show clients. In addition,
(3. change form)

artists and designers use such printers to make _____ and imaginary
(4. not real)

artistic concepts more realistic.

Three-dimensional printers are quite different from traditional methods of

printing. These printers actually create multiple _____ of material,
(5. levels)

each with a slightly different shape. The total effect is a three-dimensional

object that people can see, touch, and work with. In some cases, the objects

appear to be _____ real. Many of these machines use a type of
(6. almost)

powdered material to make 3-D objects. Because these materials are quite

different from paper, such printers must be carefully cleaned _____ .
(7. regularly)

Another major difference between 3-D printers and traditional printers is the

price. Three-dimensional printers are a relatively high-cost item.

As a noun, the word *function* means "a special activity or purpose of a person or thing."

> The main **function** of mass transit is to help people get around.

When used as a verb, *function* means "to work or operate in the correct way."

> Technology often **functions** as a way to make life easier and more convenient.

The adjective *functional* means "of or having a special activity, purpose, or task," "designed to be practical and useful with little or no decoration," or "in operation; working."

> There is a **functional** purpose to the plan as well. It's meant to make our work easier.

Functionally is an adverb which means that something is done in a practical and useful way, not necessarily an appealing one.

> The object was **functionally** perfect for the job of cleaning small printer parts—small, precise, and neat.

CORPUS

B. Circle the form of *function* that is correct in each sentence.

1. What's the more (*function* / *functional* / *functionally*) of the two choices?

2. My new exercise room serves an important (*function* / *functional* / *functionally*); it helps me keep fit.

3. The new product was (*function* / *functional* / *functionally*) very effective in that it did the job perfectly.

The word *virtual* means "being almost or nearly the thing described."

> Air traffic came to a **virtual** standstill during the storm.

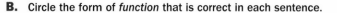

When referring to technology, *virtual* means "made to appear to exist by the use of computer programs."

> In the video game, players seemed to move around in a **virtual** world.

The adverb is *virtually*, which can be used as a synonym for *almost*.

> You can print **virtually** any small object with a 3-D printer.

CORPUS

C. Complete each sentence with either *virtual* or *virtually*.

1. The weather made it ___virtually___ impossible for us to finish painting the house this spring.

2. The most common use of _____ reality technology is in games.

3. The reunion included _____ everyone we're related to.

4. In some deserts, _____ no rain falls for years at a time.

About the Topic

Three-dimensional (3-D) design allows a person to create images in three dimensions: width, height, and depth. New printer technology now allows artists, architects, and design professionals to create actual objects from these designs.

Before You Watch

Read these questions. Discuss your answers in a small group.

1. What kinds of technology (computers, television, communication devices) do you use every day?

2. What do you know about three-dimensional (3-D) technology?

3. How do you think 3-D printers might make life easier?

Watch

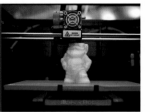

Read the Listen for Main Ideas activity below. Go online to watch a classroom discussion about 3-D printing. The students and professor are talking about the ways it is changing the printing world.

Listen for Main Ideas

Read the questions about the video. Work with a partner to ask and answer these questions.

1. What is 3-D printing and how does it work?

2. What kinds of people use 3-D printers?

3. What kinds of things can be made with 3-D printers now?

LISTENING SKILL Comparison and Contrast

LEARN

Speakers use expressions of comparison and contrast to show how ideas relate to each other. For example, comparing a new idea to a familiar idea helps listeners more easily understand the new idea. One idea may also be contrasted with another idea to show differences. The following charts, on page 29, show common comparison or contrast expressions.

Comparison expressions	
as … as	looks / seems like
both … (and)	neither … nor
in the same way	similar(ly)
like / likewise	the same as …

Contrast expressions	
although / even though	more / less … than …
but / however	not as … as
contrary to / on the contrary	on one hand / on the other hand
conversely	unlike
… is different from …	instead (of)

APPLY

A. Read the sentences. Are they comparing or contrasting information? Write *CM* (comparing) or *CT* (contrasting). Then work with a partner to identify the expressions of comparison or contrast used.

_CT_ 1. Two-dimensional (2-D) printers are not as expensive as 3-D printers.

____ 2. Engineers and architects have been using CAD for years, and likewise, artists are now using CAD with 3-D printers to create sculptures.

____ 3. Both 3-D printers and CAD programs are likely to become more popular in the future.

____ 4. The nice thing about 3-D printing is that instead of making expensive models, companies can now print out 3-D designs quickly and easily.

____ 5. The use of 3-D printing is becoming more popular, although it is still less common than 2-D printing.

B. Go online to watch the rest of the class discussion. Complete the chart with the things being compared or contrasted. Then watch again. Work with a partner to identify the comparison and contrast expressions used.

First item	Compared or contrasted	Second item
1. A 3-D scanner		a computer scanner
2. Documents	are compared to	
3.	are contrasted with	making customer-specific 3-D products
4. Artists		technical designers

C. In a small group, compare and contrast 3-D printing with traditional printing technology. Use words and phrases to cue comparisons and contrasts.

Vocabulary Activities

Word Form Chart			
Noun	**Verb**	**Adjective**	**Adverb**
consensus	consent	consenting	_____
dynamic	_____	dynamic	dynamically
_____	_____	identical	identically
precision	_____	precise	precisely
_____	_____	technical	technically

A. Read the email from an artist to a supporter. Then fill in the blanks with words from the Word Form Chart above. Use the word in parentheses to help you.

Dear Bill,

Thank you very much for supporting my art project. You asked about the name of my sculpture series, which is "Two Halves, One Whole." To be

_____precise_____ , the name actually refers to the work itself. Each piece is
(1. exact)

designed to be two _____ parts—the same shape, the same size—
(2. exactly equal)

that fit together exactly to make one sculpture. The work was very difficult

_____ because I had to use a lot of different machines and design
(3. with respect to skills)

systems to make them. It was also challenging because I had to get a letter

of _____ from the museum to make some changes to the exhibit
(4. agreement)

hall to fit the larger pieces. However, I'm happy with the results in this

_____ and think the show turned out to be very _____ and
(5. case)   (6. full of life)

exciting. Thanks again for viewing my show, and please sign up for my

newsletter. That way you can get a schedule of my upcoming exhibits.

Best,

Eric

The word *dynamic* can be used to describe things as "full of energy or ideas," "moving," or "active."

> Web developers try to create **dynamic** web content that keeps users interested.

> New clothing designers are bringing **dynamic** changes to the field of fashion.

As a noun, *dynamic* means "the way in which people or things behave and react to each other." For example, you can have a *group dynamic* that describes the way people in a particular group behave when they're together.

> Manil and his co-workers get along, help each other, and have fun together. This good group **dynamic** helps them get a lot of work done.

CORPUS

B. How is the word *dynamic* used in these phrases? Write *ADJ* (adjective) or *N* (noun). Then make sentences describing what each one might be like with a partner.

ADJ 1. a dynamic marketing team *A dynamic marketing team would have a lot of*

   friendly and outgoing people on it.

___ 2. a community dynamic _____

___ 3. a classroom dynamic _____

___ 4. a dynamic public speaker _____

___ 5. a family dynamic _____

___ 6. a dynamic personality _____

C. Look at the meanings for the word *mechanism* below. Then read the sentences. Work with a partner to decide which meaning is used in each sentence.

Meaning 1: a set of moving parts in a machine that performs a task

Meaning 2: a method or a system for achieving something

Meaning 3: a system of parts in a living thing that together perform a
particular function

_2_ 1. Psychologists call certain behaviors "defense mechanisms," such as when people get angry or afraid.

___ 2. The computer was so old its internal mechanisms could not be replaced.

___ 3. The company had a reporting mechanism in place to send updates on any problems.

___ 4. The balance mechanism in most animals is very delicate.

About the Topic

In several ways, technology has changed the ways we do business, socialize, and manage our private lives. Therefore, it's not surprising that technology has also deeply affected the art world. Today, many artists and art supporters are using technology in new ways to create, sell, and buy art.

Before You Listen

Read these questions. Discuss your answers in a small group.

1. Have you ever taken an art class? What did you learn?

2. What recent advances in technology do you think can be used to make art?

3. Which do you think requires more skill, creating art by hand or using a computer?

Listen

Read the Listen for Main Ideas activity below.
Go online to listen to an art student's presentation.
She is talking about how technology has influenced
today's art world.

Listen for Main Ideas

Read the questions about the audio. Work with a partner to ask and answer these questions.

1. In what way are artists connecting on the Internet?

2. How is technology affecting how people view famous pieces of art?

3. What kinds of art projects that use technology are described in the presentation?

SPEAKING SKILL   Summarizing Information

LEARN

Sometimes you will need to summarize a text, presentation, or video for an assignment. When summarizing include the following information:

- The main theme or topic of the piece

- A general description of the topic

- Key words or expressions, examples, reasons, and important details that support the main theme

- A summary statement of what the piece is about

Some useful language for giving summaries includes:

Introducing topics	Talking about sources	Giving supporting information	Summarizing statements
The discussion is about … The topic of the presentation / lecture / speech is … *(The speaker)* mainly talks about …	According to *(the speaker)* … *(The speaker)* says / points out / explains that …	The term ____ is used for / to … One example / reason given is … *(The speaker)* illustrates / supports this with / by …	In conclusion, *(the speaker)* seems to … Basically, … To sum things up, …

APPLY

A. Listen to the excerpts from presentations. Write the number of the excerpt next to the correct summary.

____ The lecturer mainly talks about digital media and how video is used to create art. He says that digital media has become the new paintbrush and canvas in the art world. One example he gives is an artist who creates installations using buses and video. The term *installation* is used to talk about when artists create a special environment. In conclusion, the speaker seems to be an expert in digital art.

____ The topic of the lecture is how technology is helping make art more available to people. The speaker illustrates this with several examples including a museum that lets viewers buy digital prints "on demand," which means they can buy them any time. To sum things up, she feels technology is important because it offers several useful ways to share beauty.

B. Read the summaries in activity A again. With a partner, circle the summarizing expressions.

C. Listen to another excerpt from a presentation. Summarize what the speaker is saying in three sentences or less.

_____

_____

_____

_____

D. Go online to listen to the original student's presentation. Prepare a 30-second summary to present to a partner. Use expressions for summarizing.

LEARN

Effective speakers chunk their speech, stress important information, pause between main ideas, and signal when they have finished—or not finished—a thought. In writing, this is done with punctuation: commas, dashes, periods, semi-colons, and colons. In speech, this is done with chunking, pausing, sentence focus, and intonation.

A. Go online to listen to a student express frustration about a programming assignment. Listen for the focus words. They will stand out because the speaker lengthens them.

APPLY

A. Go online and listen to the student again. Mark (|) where he pauses. Circle the stressed focus word in each chunk between pauses.

I've been working on (this) | for (hours) and I'm totally stuck I keep getting the

same error message over and over and I don't understand what it means I

tried to fix it but then I got even more error messages Now it just seems to

be getting worse and worse and I'm tearing my hair out This thing is due

tomorrow and I'm ready to throw my computer out the window

B. Go online and listen again. Listen carefully to the last word in each chunk. Does the speaker use falling intonation to signal the end of a thought or rising intonation to indicate that he has more to say? Check the intonation pattern you hear. Then discuss your answers with a partner.

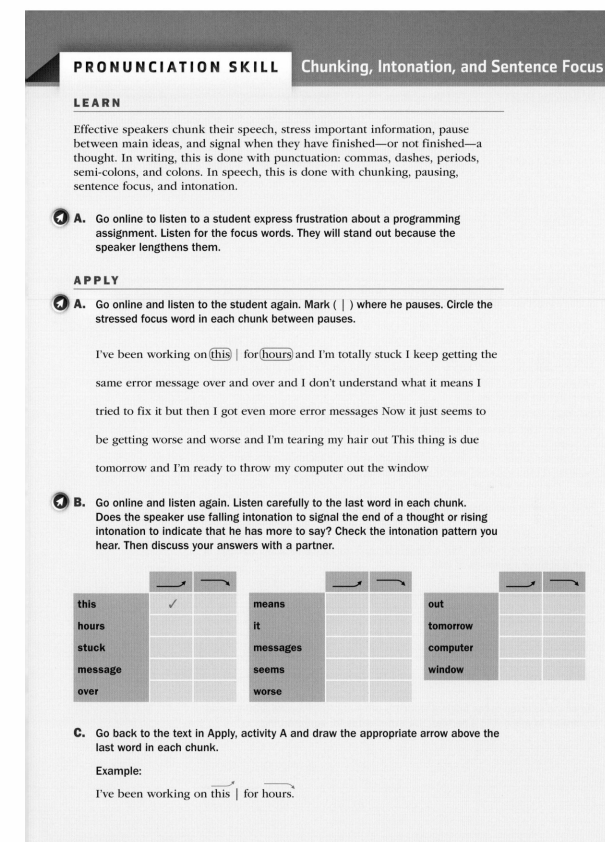

	↗	↘		↗	↘		↗	↘
this	✓		means			out		
hours			it			tomorrow		
stuck			messages			computer		
message			seems			window		
over			worse					

C. Go back to the text in Apply, activity A and draw the appropriate arrow above the last word in each chunk.

Example:

I've been working on this | for hours.

D. Work with a partner. Say the text in Apply, activity A aloud. Monitor chunking, pausing, sentence focus, and intonation. Give immediate feedback. Then switch roles.

> A: *I've been working on* **this**.
>
> B: *Stress "working."*
>
> A: *I've been* **working** *on this.*
>
> B: *Nice. Now go up at the end of the chunk.*
>
> A: *I've been* **working** *on this.*
>
> B: *Sounds good. Now make it smoother.*
>
> A: *I've been* **working** *on this.*

End of Unit Task

In this unit, you learned how to recognize compared and contrasted information and give a summary of what's been said. Review these skills by noting the comparisons and contrasts in a conversation and then giving a summary of the speaker's views.

 A. Go online to listen to an interview with two people. Work with a partner to identify the main theme they are talking about. Write a general description of the topic.

 B. Listen again and note the similarities, differences, and other details the two people talk about.

Similarities	Differences
Key words, examples, reasons, and details	

C. Compare your notes with a partner. Identify the main points each person makes.

Jessica	Samer

D. Work with a partner to come up with one sentence that summarizes the conversation.

E. Work with a partner to create a short presentation summarizing the similarities and differences between the ways that the two speakers use 3-D printers for their work. Use the comparison, contrast, and summary language you learned in the unit. Share your presentations in small groups.

Self-Assessment		
Yes	**No**	
☐	☐	I successfully identified expressions for comparing and contrasting information.
☐	☐	I was able to match complete presentations, discussions, and lectures with summaries of the information.
☐	☐	I was able to give a 30-second summary of the complete presentation about how technology is influencing the art world.
☐	☐	I can chunk my speech, highlight important information, pause between main ideas, and signal when I have finished or not finished a thought.
☐	☐	I can correctly use the target vocabulary words from the unit.

Discussion Questions

With a partner or in a small group, discuss the following questions.

1. Why would a designer want to print a small 3-D model of a larger item (such as a building) before building the real thing?

2. How could you use a 3-D printer at home?

3. What types of things could you NOT use a 3-D printer to build?

4

The Virus Game

In this unit, you will

> learn about research involving virtual viruses.
> increase your understanding of the target academic words for this unit.

LISTENING AND SPEAKING SKILLS

> Figurative Language
> Using Idioms to Engage Your Audience
> **PRONUNCIATION** Stress in Phrasal Verbs

Self-Assessment

Think about how well you know each target word, and check (✓) the appropriate column. I have…

TARGET WORDS	never seen this word before.	heard or seen the word but am not sure what it means.	heard or seen the word and understand what it means.	used the word confidently in *either* speaking or writing.
AWL				
accumulate				
🔑 contract				
ethic				
furthermore				
hypothesis				
incidence				
insight				
likewise				
🔑 monitor				
🔑 obtain				
parameter				
persist				
reinforce				
simulate				

🔑 Oxford 3000™ keywords

Vocabulary Activities

The noun *contract* means "an official written, legal agreement."

*I'm signing a new **contract** today, so I can stay in my apartment for another year.*

The verb *contract* has several meanings. *Contract* can mean "to make a written, legal agreement with someone," "become or make something become less or smaller," or "get an illness or disease."

*They're in the process of **contracting** a new real estate agent to sell their house.*

*When you stretch your chest you can feel your back muscles **contract**.*

*While he was on vacation, he **contracted** the flu.*

 CORPUS

A. Some words have multiple meanings. For the word *contract*, match each dictionary definition on the left with the correct example sentence on the right.

> contract (noun, verb)

Definitions

_b_ 1. a written, legal agreement

___ 2. to make a written, legal agreement with someone

___ 3. to become or make something become smaller or shorter

___ 4. to get an illness or disease

Example Sentences

a. When you get cold, your blood vessels contract, which helps to keep you warm.

b. When the player signed the contract, he agreed to stay with the team for two years.

c. More than 40 percent of students contracted the virus during last year's flu season.

d. We loved our neighbor's kitchen remodel so much, we contracted the same company to do ours.

B. Read these excerpts from a lecture about public health. In each sentence, circle the word or phrase in parentheses that has the same meaning as the underlined word in the sentence. Compare your answers with a partner.

1. One factor that many students worry about is the <u>accumulation</u> (*advance* / (*build-up*) / *amount*) of loans to pay for college.

2. A team of researchers at the Monterey Institute of Health <u>monitored</u> (*tracked* / *described* / *reduced*) college students' daily usage of laptops and desktop computers.

3. Computer simulations give scientists <u>insight into</u> (*understanding of* / *thoughts about* / *fear of*) how diseases spread in the real world.

4. Animals can carry viruses. <u>Likewise</u>, (*However* / *Of course* / *As well*) people can carry viruses.

5. In order to <u>obtain</u> (*purchase / renew / get*) a vaccine, people usually go to their local hospital.

6. It was a rare <u>incident</u> (*situation / party / trial*) to have a cobra escape from the zoo.

C. Put each word in the box in the correct column under the target word it is a synonym for. Use your dictionary to check word meanings as needed.

assumption	comprehension	guideline	possibility
awareness	earn	idea	secure
be given	framework	judgment	theory
boundary	get hold of	limit	understanding

hypothesis	insight	obtain	parameter
_____	_____	*be given*	_____
_____	_____	_____	_____
_____	_____	_____	_____
_____	_____	_____	_____

D. Write the word from the box that works best as a topic for each list. Then add one more example to the end of each list.

accumulate	contract	ethical	monitor	obtain

1. __*accumulate*__ : wealth, power, information, __*money*__

2. _____ : progress, changes, events, _____

3. _____ : permission, permits, information, _____

4. _____ : issues, dilemma, behavior, _____

5. _____ : an illness, a virus, an employee, _____

E. Read the sentences. Write the correct part of speech (noun, verb, etc.) for the bold word in each sentence.

1. The doctor gave **insightful** advice to her patient. __*adjective*__

2. If you don't get a vaccine before you travel, you could **contract** an illness.
_____

3. Social video games can provide **insight** into how people interact in real life.
_____

About the Topic

Viruses are living things that are too small to be seen with the naked eye. They cause diseases in other living things. Scientists often use computer simulations to model how diseases spread. Online video games with many players are a type of simulated world, too.

Before You Listen

Read these questions. Discuss your answers in a small group.

1. Do you know how software is used in a computer system? Explain briefly.

2. When people around you are sick, what do you do to stay healthy?

3. What are some factors that allow viruses to spread?

Listen

Read the Listen for Main Ideas activity below. Go online to listen to an interview about virtual viruses. An author discusses a way scientists used video games to learn about how live viruses spread.

Listen for Main Ideas

Read the questions about the interview. Work with a partner to ask and answer these questions.

1. How did Dr. Fefferman learn about how diseases spread?

2. What are similarities between how a virus spreads in a game and in the real world?

3. How does curiosity influence the spread of disease?

4. What have public health officials learned from the "Corrupted Blood Incident"?

LISTENING SKILL   Figurative Language

LEARN

Figurative language expresses an idea different from the actual meaning of the words used. Idioms are one example of figurative language. Your instructor may ask you to learn a grammar rule "by heart." The idiom *learn* (something) *by heart* means "memorize something." This phrase is figurative language because, of course, we don't literally use our hearts to learn; we use our minds.

Follow these steps to listen for figurative language.

1. Think about the meaning of the words you hear.

   For example, in the panel discussion, the moderator said, "How can a video game give us insight into how diseases spread? We hope to get to the bottom of the mystery today."

2. Identify the language that isn't used literally.

   In this example, a mystery is not a physical object, so it doesn't have a "top" or a "bottom."

3. Ask yourself a question using the figurative language.

   For example, "Does a mystery have a bottom?" In this case, the answer is no because the phrase *get to the bottom of something* is an idiom.

4. Look at the context of whole sentence to guess the figurative meaning of the phrase. Use an idiom dictionary or the Internet to help you find the meaning.

   In this example, *get to the bottom of* something means "understand the cause of something."

APPLY

A. Use the context of each sentence to understand the idiom. Match each idiom on the left (underlined) to its meaning on the right.

_b_ 1. Jason had to leave work early today. He was feeling <u>under the weather</u>.   a. a nervous feeling

___ 2. When I think I'm <u>coming down with something</u>, I always try to rest and take vitamins.   b. ill, sick

___ 3. Before my presentation, my hands were shaking, and I had <u>butterflies in my stomach</u>.   c. strong pain in the head

___ 4. I can't meet with you today because I have a <u>splitting headache</u>.   d. beginning to feel sick

B. Go online to listen to the first half of the interview again. Complete the idioms you hear. Discuss the figurative meaning of the idioms with a partner.

1. A professor at Tufts University ___*took an*___ interest in the incident.

   Meaning: became interested in

2. That's the heart of _____, isn't it?

3. It really _____ a life of its own.

4. They _____ of criticism from their players.

5. They become carriers of the illness that way. Curiosity _____, you know?

C. Go online to listen to the rest of the interview. List other idioms you hear. Work in a small group. Use the context to determine what each idiom means.

Vocabulary Activities

Word Form Chart			
Noun	**Verb**	**Adjective**	**Adverb**
_____	_____	_____	furthermore
persistence	persist	persistent	persistently
reinforcement	reinforce	reinforced	_____
simulation	simulate	simulated	_____

A. Read the story about a new technology that's helping patients. Fill in each blank with the appropriate word from the Word Form Chart.

When patients kept calling Dr. Maria Lucia Hernandez's office, she had to

reinforce her two main rules: leave a message and wait patiently. Why? In
(1)

her small, rural town, most patients had no cars. _____, the town had
(2)

no public transportation. Dr. Hernandez spent most of her day making house

calls. She was the only doctor for miles, so she spent up to three hours per

day driving and visiting patients. But that's changed now.

A new system called VirtuDoc is helping Dr. Hernandez serve her patients

better. Now she _____ many of her office visits using a computer
(3)

technology. A grant helped to pay for her workstation and workstations

around the community. The technology has helped her treat hundreds of

patients. Local residents are able to sit in front of a web camera and have

Dr. Hernandez give them advice over the Internet. "Sometimes it's clear that

there's a serious problem," Dr. Hernandez explains. "Then I usually ask

them to come in to my office. Sometimes they don't want to come in, but I'm

_____."
(4)

With so many _____ office visits, Dr. Hernandez spends less time
(5)

driving and more time helping people. "I am able to spend more time with

patients. It _____ my belief that face-to-face time with patients should
(6)

be quality time. _____, the office visits become more focused on
(7)

major troubles patients have. They get better care."

These office-visit _____ are improving patient care in another big
(8)

way. Access to the Internet means doctors from other places can give second

opinions to her patients. "It's nice to have some _____ from other
(9)

doctors. Thanks to this new system, my patients have access to other great

doctors," Dr. Hernandez explains. "Now we can all serve our patients better."

Incidence is a singular noun that means "the extent to which something
(usually something bad) happens" or "the rate of something." *Incidence*
often collocates with the preposition *of*.

> Increased public education has led to a lower **incidence of** flu in schools.

> The **incidence of** drought in our country is something that concerns us all.

An *incident* is an event (especially one that involves danger or something
unusual). *Incidentally* is used to introduce extra news or information that the
speaker just thought of or that may be unrelated to the topic of discussion.

> We're glad the driver was not injured in the **incident**.

> I'm meeting with Dr. Fought today. **Incidentally**, she and I went to college
> together.

CORPUS

B. Read the sentences and write the correct form of *incidence*.

1. Wearing sunscreen reduces the ___*incidence*___ of skin cancer in adults.

2. The day after Dimitry argued with his friend, he apologized for the
   _____ .

3. Optometrists are seeing a higher _____ of certain vision problems
   because of computer use.

4. I usually make a chocolate cake for my son's birthday, which, _____,
   is tomorrow.

About the Topic

Scientists work hard to find cures for serious illnesses, such as cancer and
tuberculosis. Researchers have long been studying the bacterium that causes
tuberculosis, a serious disease that especially affects the lungs. They only
recently learned where it hides in the body.

Before You Watch

Read these questions. Discuss your answers in a small group.

1. How do scientists and other people experiment and make new discoveries?

2. Do you think advances in medical knowledge are always positive? Why or why not?

3. What scientific discoveries have helped or been useful to you?

Watch

Read the Listen for Main Ideas activity below. Go online to watch a classroom discussion about scientific discoveries.

Listen for Main Ideas

Read the questions about the video. Work with a partner to ask and answer these questions.

1. What is one example of a surprise scientific discovery?

2. How does the student with a cousin in England feel about Britain's reaction to hoof and mouth disease?

3. Why does one student want to work in the public health sector?

4. What important discovery was made about tuberculosis?

SPEAKING SKILL   Using Idioms to Engage Your Audience

LEARN

Idioms are commonly used in English. An idiom is a group of words whose meaning is different from the meanings of the individual words. Idioms are not formal language. However, because they give an idea in an informal way, they can help to make your speech interesting.

For example, *be on pins and needles* means "be very worried about something." In the video, a speaker says, "In situations where people used to be on pins and needles, science is helping people feel more relaxed." If people are no longer on pins and needles, then they are no longer very worried. But "They were on pins and needles" is a more interesting phrase than "They were worried."

One way to engage your audience, or keep their attention, is to use interesting language. Idioms can help.

A. Choose the correct meaning for the underlined idiom. Then discuss the idioms with a partner.

1. My grandfather is 90 years old, but he is still <u>fit as a fiddle</u>. He still works around the house and walks in the park every afternoon.

   a. tall and thin

   b. in good health

   c. has good eyesight

2. I've been feeling tired all day and now my throat is sore. I think I may be <u>coming down with something</u>. If you don't see me in class tomorrow, you'll know why.

   a. becoming ill

   b. cooking for a friend

   c. planning a vacation

3. I really <u>put my foot in my mouth</u> with Alicia. I told her she looked great and asked if she had lost weight. She said she's been sick for three weeks.

   a. give a compliment

   b. offer unwanted advice

   c. accidentally say something rude

B. Watch the discussion again. Listen for idioms. Complete the following idioms. Then work with a partner. Use each idiom in a sentence.

1. _____hoping_____ against hope

2. get _____ game

3. keep my _____

4. _____ rid _____

5. make no bones _____

C. Brainstorm with your class. Write idioms you know, with the meanings, on the board. Discuss the meanings of the idioms.

D. Practice using idioms. Work with a partner. Ask each other questions, using idioms the class brainstormed for activity C.

LEARN

Two- and three-word verbs follow a very reliable stress rule: stress the particle. The particle is the part of the phrase that looks like a preposition.

A. Go online to listen to phrasal verbs. Notice that the stress is on the second word.

1. fight off	4. go around	7. end up
2. hang on	5. wipe out	8. knock out
3. pick up	6. speed up	9. come down (with)

Phrasal verbs have a shifting pattern that depends on where they are in a sentence.

1. When a phrasal verb comes at the end of a chunk, stress the second word.
2. When a phrasal verb comes at the beginning or in the middle of a chunk, shift the stress to the first word.

B. Go online to listen to the difference between stress patterns. Notice where the phrasal verb is in the sentence.

I'm fighting off | a sore throat.	Have you managed | to fight off that cold?
This new bug | really knocks you out.	What are you taking | to knock out that flu?

C. The stress in three-word phrasal verbs does not usually change. Go online to listen to these sentences.

I hope | you're not coming down | with the flu!	What have you come down with?

APPLY

A. Go online. Listen and repeat the verbs in Learn, activity A. Stress the second word.

B. Practice the sentences in Learn, activities B and C. Pay attention to shifting stress.

C. Go online to listen to the dialogue. The phrasal verbs are underlined. Circle the stressed word in each phrasal verb.

A: Have you managed | to (fight) off that cold?

B: No, | not really. | It's still hanging on. | I can't seem | to get rid of this cough.

A: *Actually, | I think I'm <u>fighting off</u> | a sore throat. | I must've <u>picked it up</u> at work.*

B: *There's a lot of that | <u>going around</u>.*

A: *Are you also feeling completely exhausted? | My body aches | all over.*

B: *Uh-oh … | I hope | you're not <u>coming down</u> | <u>with</u> the flu! | I hear this new one | really <u>wipes</u> you <u>out</u>. | What are you taking for it?*

D. Practice the dialogue with a partner.

End of Unit Task

In a small group, you will research three idioms and teach them to the class. Then you will perform a short skit using your idioms. While your classmates perform, you will have the chance to listen for figurative language.

A. Form a small group. Choose three idioms from this list.

Idioms	
a show of hands	at the drop of a hat
bite your tongue	go back to square one
break a leg	go the extra mile
don't quit your day job	hold your horses
everything but the kitchen sink	it's a piece of cake

B. Write your three idioms. Use your dictionary or the Internet to help you find the meanings of your idioms.

Idiom	Meaning

C. Discuss the meaning and use of your idioms. Check that all members of your group understand them and are comfortable using them in conversation.

D. Write example sentences using the idioms. Be prepared to share these with your classmates.

1. _____

2. _____

3. _____

E. Think of a situation in which all three of your idioms might be used. Work with your group to create a short skit that uses all three idioms. Try to use at least three target vocabulary words from this unit in your skit.

F. Teach your idioms to the class and perform your skit.

G. While your classmates perform, listen for the idioms in their speech. Write down idioms you hear and guess the meaning from the context of the skit.

_____

_____

_____

H. After each group performs a skit, review the idiom meanings as a class.

Discuss:

1. Which performer used the idioms?
2. What was the situation that each idiom was used in?
3. What is the meaning of each idiom?

Self-Assessment		
Yes	**No**	
☐	☐	I successfully recognized idioms in an audio clip.
☐	☐	I successfully used three idioms in a skit.
☐	☐	I used at least three target vocabulary words from the unit in my skit.
☐	☐	I used appropriate stress in phrasal verbs.
☐	☐	I can correctly use the target vocabulary words from the unit.

Discussion Questions

With a partner or in a small group, discuss the following questions.

1. How are computer viruses like real diseases?
2. Why do scientists study computer viruses?
3. What makes a video go viral?

Recording Our Lives

In this unit, you will
> learn about viral Internet videos.
> increase your understanding of the target academic words for this unit.

LISTENING AND SPEAKING SKILLS
> Listening for Details
> Making a Concise Presentation
> **PRONUNCIATION** Stress in Phrasal Verbs and Nouns

Self-Assessment
Think about how well you know each target word, and check (✓) the appropriate column. I have…

TARGET WORDS	never seen this word before.	heard or seen the word but am not sure what it means.	heard or seen the word and understand what it means.	used the word confidently in *either* speaking *or* writing.
AWL				
🔑 appropriate				
assign				
attain				
🔑 capable				
🔑 cycle				
🔑 debate				
🔑 emerge				
🔑 formula				
🔑 logic				
🔑 nevertheless				
🔑 notion				
refine				
subsequent				
🔑 technique				

🔑 Oxford 3000™ keywords

Vocabulary Activities

<table>
<tr><th colspan="4">Word Form Chart</th></tr>
<tr><th>Noun</th><th>Verb</th><th>Adjective</th><th>Adverb</th></tr>
<tr><td>appropriateness</td><td>_____</td><td>appropriate</td><td>appropriately</td></tr>
<tr><td>attainment</td><td>attain</td><td>attainable</td><td>_____</td></tr>
<tr><td>capability</td><td>_____</td><td>capable</td><td>capably</td></tr>
<tr><td>technique</td><td>_____</td><td>_____</td><td>_____</td></tr>
</table>

A. Complete the paragraph using the correct forms of the words in the Word Form Chart. Check your answers with a partner. Use the words in parentheses to help you.

YouTube is a video sharing website that is changing the world. Over the years, more and more people have been posting videos to YouTube. They hope that they will become very popular and "go viral," or be shared by millions. Because of the popularity of these videos, various businesses are now hoping to use viral videos as a marketing ___technique___. They are
(1. method)
making interesting and creative videos that they want people to share with everyone they know. If people send them on to all their friends and family, the videos will _____ "viral" status. Many companies are now using
(2. reach)
this type of marketing with some success. However, people are still not sure as to whether it is a(n) _____ marketing style for most businesses.
(3. correct)
The key to its success will be whether marketing firms are _____ of
(4. able)
consistently making videos that appeal to everyone.

The word *assign* can be used in two ways depending on whether it refers to a thing or a person. When the direct object is a thing, *assign* means "to give something to someone for a particular purpose."

*The instructor **assigned** extra exercises to help us practice using irregular verbs.*

When the direct object is a person, *assign* means "to give someone a particular job or type of work to do."

*My supervisor **assigned** me to the new linguistics research project that starts next month.*

The noun form of *assign* is *assignment*. This means "a task or piece of work that somebody is given to do, usually as part of their job or studies."

*Our **assignment** was to give a presentation about a topic that interested us.*

CORPUS

B. Read each sentence and decide which meaning is used. Write 1, 2, or 3.

Meaning 1: to give something to someone for a particular purpose

Meaning 2: to give someone a particular job or type of work to do

Meaning 3: a task or piece of work that somebody is given to do

_1_ 1. Many colleges try to assign students a roommate based on their similar interests.

____ 2. Companies often assign new employees small tasks to test capability.

____ 3. Sometimes it's difficult to explain the scores the judges assign to different performers.

____ 4. The assignment was to write about a famous author, but she wrote about a famous inventor instead.

C. Write the synonyms of the target words in the correct columns. Use a dictionary as needed. Compare your answers with a partner.

appear	belief	idea
argue	come up	talk about
become known	discuss	thought

debate	emerge	notion
_____	_appear_	_____
_____	_____	_____
_____	_____	_____

About the Topic

Viral videos are a form of media that has become very popular. When a video "goes viral," it is forwarded or shared by more and more people until it's seen by millions. Because of this popularity, marketing firms are now turning to viral videos as a form of advertising.

Before You Watch

Read these questions. Discuss your answers in a small group.

1. Have you ever recorded a video? If so, what did you record?
2. What kinds of pictures, videos, or messages on the Internet do you and your friends find interesting?
3. What kinds of videos (if any) have people shared with you?

Watch

Read the Listen for Main Ideas activity below. Go online to watch a marketing professor's lecture. He talks about the use of viral video for advertising and promotion.

Listen for Main Ideas

Read the questions about the lecture. Circle the correct answers. Then work with a partner to ask and answer these questions. Discuss why the other answer options are incorrect.

1. Which topic <u>doesn't</u> the professor mention?
   a. why people share videos
   b. the history of viral video
   c. how to make a successful viral video
2. What is the professor's general attitude about viral videos in marketing?
   a. It's exciting but uncertain.
   b. It's a trend that won't be around for long.
   c. Viral videos have a long and successful history as marketing tools.
3. What is the future of viral video?
   a. It is on its way out.
   b. We don't know yet.
   c. It has reached its full potential.

LISTENING SKILL   Listening for Details

LEARN

You may need to recall detailed information that supports the main idea of a lecture or presentation. Before you listen, ask yourself, "What will I do with the information I hear? Write a report? Take a test? Give a summary?" Then think about the types of details needed to successfully complete the task. When you know the purpose of your listening, you can listen more effectively. Listen for words that signal important or specific information:

Kind of information	What to listen for
Specific words and definitions	Signal words: The term *X* means ... ; *X* refers to ... ;
Names, dates, or data	The repetition or spelling of important information: That's Martin Kale, K-A-L-E. **Years or dates:** March 6th, 1995 **Words that signal data:** According to *(a recent study)* ... ; Research indicates ...
Examples	Signal words: For example; For instance; ... such as ... ; **If a speaker gives an example without using a signal word, it usually comes just before or after the main idea:** Many nature documentaries have been successful including *March of the Penguins* and *African Cats*.
Reasons	Signal words: ... so ... ; because *(of this)*; ... since **If a speaker gives reasons without using signal words, they may be listed immediately following the topic.** Film students enjoy what they do. It's a fun career.

APPLY

A. Go online to listen to the statements about jobs in film studies. What details is the person giving? Write the detail type. Then listen again and note the signal words used (if any). Discuss your answers with a partner.

1. **detail:** _____*reason*_____ **signal word:** _____*since*_____

2. **detail:** _____ **signal word:** _____

3. **detail:** _____ **signal word:** _____

B. Read the questions and note the information needed to answer them. Then go online to listen to parts of a film study lecture to find the answers.

1. What are two reasons film studies are popular right now?

2. What example of a successful video does the speaker give and how many views did it receive?

C. Work with a partner to decide what information you need to answer the questions. Watch the lecture again and answer questions.

1. For what meaning do people often use the term *viral video*?
   _____*specific word, definition*_____

2. From what year to what year did accidental filming make up most of the viral video content? _____

3. What types of videos are mentioned as examples of the more organized approach to going viral? _____

Vocabulary Activities

Word Form Chart			
Noun	**Verb**	**Adjective**	**Adverb**
cycle	cycle	cyclical	_____
logic	_____	logical	logically
refinement	refine	refined	_____
_____	_____	subsequent	subsequently

A. Fill in the blanks with the correct form of a target word in the Word Form Chart. Use your dictionary as needed. Compare answers with a partner.

1. No viral video is likely to be funny forever. To stay fresh, people are always

   trying to ____refine____ their jokes and appeal to new audiences.

(make better)

2. I was finally able to get my camera fixed and _____ made the

(later)

   deadline for the photo contest.

3. One _____ way to improve the marketing plan would be to do a

(sensible)

   survey about why people share videos. That will get us the information we

   need to know.

Formula is a noun that has a few definitions. In math and science, it means "a group of signs, letters, or numbers used to express a rule or a law" or "a list of substances used for making something." *Formula* can also refer to a plan or "a particular method of doing or achieving something."

> H_2O is the chemical **formula** for water.

> The restaurant kept its **formula** for making barbeque sauce a secret.

> The soccer team needs a new **formula** for winning games.

Formulate is a verb that means "to create or prepare carefully."

> To win the debate, Maxine needs to **formulate** better arguments.

Formulation is a noun that means "the action of creating or preparing something."

> The **formulation** of a university curriculum is not an easy process.

CORPUS

B. Write the correct form of the word *formula* to complete each phrase. Notice the surrounding words. Then work with a partner to make complete sentences.

1. ___*formulate*___ a plan

2. the _____ for a new soft drink

3. policy _____

4. an interesting _____

5. _____ an excuse

6. the original _____

The word *nevertheless* is an adverb that means "despite something that you have just mentioned." While it is similar to *however* and *but* in meaning, it is more formal and may often be used with either word.

> *I didn't want to enjoy the video; <u>however</u>, I ended up liking it* **nevertheless**.

Nevertheless is often used when contrasting information or admitting a point. It can be placed in the initial position of a sentence or clause or at the end when used with *however* or *but*.

> *I know there are good reasons to do business on the Internet.* **Nevertheless**, *I won't put my business online.*

> *The situation at the office has improved significantly.* **Nevertheless**, *there are still a number of problems to be solved.*

> *We said we would never agree to go to the conference, <u>but</u> we decided to go* **nevertheless**.

CORPUS

C. Work with a partner. Restate each sentence, using *nevertheless* to emphasize the point.

1. We didn't want to buy the product. We bought it anyway.

2. We knew our project wouldn't do well, but I was upset that we lost.

3. TV commercials may now seem a bit dated; however, they are still a popular form of advertising.

4. She's not a very good television producer. She gets a lot of great projects.

5. There was a great documentary on Channel 4 last night at 11:00 p.m. I went to bed early because I had to work today.

6. My parents didn't want me to study film, but they paid for my education.

D. Work with a partner. Restate the sentences using the correct form of the word *cycle*, *formula*, or *refine* to replace the underlined words.

1. The company <u>made the</u> product <u>cleaner</u>.

   The company refined the product.

2. It's always the same <u>order of things happening</u>: we go on vacation, something goes wrong, we come home early.

3. There's no special <u>mixture</u> that we use to make our cakes. It's just a standard recipe.

4. We have got to <u>come up with</u> a better plan for how to proceed.

5. It's really important to <u>revise the details on</u> your report before you turn it in.

6. She usually <u>rides her bike</u> to work when the weather is nice.

About the Topic

Viral videos are popular for several reasons, but there are certain key ways that they can get and keep people's attention. In marketing, companies often use humor and emotion to influence viewers to share the videos. By making people laugh and feel good, a viral marketing video creates a good feeling about a product that makes people want to buy it.

Before You Listen

Read these questions. Discuss your answers in a small group.

1. What qualities do you think make a video interesting or appealing?
2. Have you ever written a review for a product? If so, describe your review.
3. How can emotion influence the decisions that people make?

Listen

Read the Listen for Main Ideas activity below. Go online to listen to a marketing presentation. The presentation discusses why people like viral videos and why they can make us buy products.

Listen for Main Ideas

Read the questions about the presentation. Work with a partner to ask and answer these questions.

1. In the presenter's opinion, what do effective ads do?
2. What are the two types of viral videos discussed?
3. How can you be a smart consumer?

SPEAKING SKILL Making a Concise Presentation

LEARN

In a concise presentation, the speaker uses as few words as possible to make clear statements. To speak concisely in general, you must:

- be well prepared and organized.
- state examples and supporting ideas briefly.
- include only information that is closely related to your topic.
- avoid giving too many personal opinions and asides.

At the sentence level, make sentences concise by using shorter, more direct expressions like the following:

In a situation in which this happens ... → *When* this happens ...

It's important that we discuss the plan. → We *need to* discuss the plan.

A. Make these sentences more concise. Work with a partner to rephrase the underlined expressions using the words in the box.

although	as	because	if	about

1. <u>In the event that</u> you cannot see the show, please do read the book as it's an excellent story.

   If you cannot see the show, please do read the book as it's an excellent story.

2. One shouldn't decide a film is a success only <u>owing to the fact that</u> it has won awards.

3. <u>Despite the fact that</u> many people don't like the director, the documentary did well.

4. The article was written just <u>at the same time as</u> the event occurred.

5. They needed to talk to him <u>in reference to</u> the date of the meeting.

B. Make the beginning of this presentation more concise. Cross out at least five sentences that should be deleted or changed.

Hi, everyone. Good morning! How are you all feeling today? Good, I hope.

Thank you for your attention, and I'm glad to have the opportunity to speak

with you. My presentation today is a review of the documentary *Regal*

Eagle. It's a recent production by director Slade Green. It's done quite well

with the critics, but there are some who don't think it's his best work, but

that's up to the viewers I guess. Regardless of the fact that it was not so well

received publically, I liked the film. It was funny, original, well written, and

generally nicely done. Nevertheless, there were some weak points, and I'll

be discussing them as well. I won't get into too much detail though as we're

limited on time, but I hope to give you a nice general overview of why I feel

the film is a success.

C. Go online to listen to a new version of the presentation in activity B. Listen for the changes and confirm that you understand them. Did the speaker make the same changes you did?

D. Now go online and listen to the new presentation again. Work with a partner to create a one-minute summary of the presentation. Use the techniques listed above to keep it concise. Take turns giving your presentation to two other students.

LEARN

Some phrasal verbs have a noun form. Recognizing parts of speech can help you know which word to stress when using these phrases.

Go online to listen to the stress patterns in the following verbs and nouns. Stress the second word in phrasal verbs. Move the stress to the first word for noun forms.

Phrasal verbs	Noun forms
pop up	pop-up
start up	start-up
take off	takeoff
take out	takeout
work out	workout

APPLY

A. Go online to listen to the following words in short conversations. Circle the stress pattern you hear.

	Verb	Noun
1.	back up	(backup)
2.	log in	log-in
3.	set up	setup
4.	clean up	cleanup

B. Work with a partner. Student A: Choose a phrasal verb or a noun form from the chart in Learn. Use it in a sentence, making the stress pattern easy to hear. Student B: Tell your partner whether you heard the verb or the noun. Then switch roles.

Student A: It's irritating when ads pop up on my computer.

Student B: I heard the verb "pop up."

C. Find a new partner. Student A: Say a phrase from the left column in the chart below. Student B: Listen and give the sentence in the right column that matches. Then switch roles.

Student A: Printout.

Student B: I need a printout of this.

a. print out b. printout	Can you print out this document? I need a printout of this.
a. warm up b. warm-up	Let's warm up before we go for a run. Let's start with a quick warm-up.
a. check out b. checkout	You can pay for that when you check out. You can pay with a credit card at checkout.
a. hang out b. hangout	Do you want to hang out this weekend? I know a café that's a great hangout.
a. hand out b. handout	Can you hand out these papers for me? I'm going to miss class tomorrow. Can you get the handouts?
a. mix up b. mix-up	I always mix up those two grammar points. I'm terribly sorry … There's been a mix-up with your order.
a. show off b. showoff	Don't hold back in a job interview. You have to really show off your talents! Don't be such a showoff!

End of Unit Task

Practice being concise by creating a review of a movie, documentary, or other show you have seen recently. Listen for details in your classmate's reviews.

A. Think about a film, show, or video that you have seen recently. The questions below are about details you need to include in your presentation. Note the types of information from the box needed to answer them.

date	definition	example	name	reason	data	word

1. What's the name of the film? _____

2. What does the title mean? _____

3. When did the film come out? _____

4. Who are the main characters? _____

5. Give a brief synopsis of the plot. _____

_____

B. Create your review. If you're speaking concisely, you should be able to include all the information above in a two- to three-minute speech.

C. Present your review to the class. When others are giving their presentations, listen for details.

D. Ask and answer questions about details from each presentation. Then give each speaker feedback on his / her presentation. Was it concise? Did it include enough useful details?

Self-Assessment		
Yes	**No**	
☐	☐	I successfully found the information needed to answer the questions about the viral marketing lecture.
☐	☐	I successfully revised long, unnecessary phrases in the presentation.
☐	☐	I was able to summarize the key points of the consumer presentation and keep it concise.
☐	☐	I can correctly pronounce phrasal verbs.
☐	☐	I can correctly use the target vocabulary words from the unit.

Discussion Questions

With a partner or in a small group, discuss the following questions.

1. Why do some videos go viral? What key features do they have in common?

2. What is a video you could watch over and over?

3. Do you think most viral videos happen "by accident" or are designed to go viral?

Beyond Earth

In this unit, you will
> learn about commercial space flight.
> increase your understanding of the target academic words for this unit.

LISTENING AND SPEAKING SKILLS
> Annotating Lecture Notes
> Signaling the End of a Speech
> PRONUNCIATION Shifting Stress in Two-Syllable Words

Self-Assessment
Think about how well you know each target word, and check (✓) the appropriate column. I have…

TARGET WORDS	never seen this word before.	heard or seen the word but am not sure what it means.	heard or seen the word and understand what it means.	used the word confidently in *either* speaking or writing.
AWL				
accommodate				
allocate				
🔑 classic				
conform				
cooperate				
🔑 despite				
differentiate				
facilitate				
🔑 finance				
hence				
intervene				
revenue				
straightforward				
successor				

🔑 Oxford 3000™ keywords

Vocabulary Activities

Word Form Chart			
Noun	**Verb**	**Adjective**	**Adverb**
accommodation	accommodate	accommodating	_____
conformity conformist	conform	conformable	_____
facilitation, facilitator, facility	facilitate	_____	_____
finances	finance	financial	financially
intervention	intervene	intervening	_____
successor	_____	successive	successively

A. Read the article about how space exploration is changing. Fill in each blank with the appropriate word from the Word Form Chart. Use the words in parentheses to help you.

Space exploration is changing. Until recently, governments ___*facilitated*___ all
                                                                (1. aided)

space programs. Public money helped pay for shuttles, which are vehicles

designed to transport people between Earth and space. Now, private

companies are _____ everyone's dream of traveling in space. For a
                   (2. helping)

modest _____ investment, private citizens can experience space flight.
          (3. fiscal)

Each shuttle can _____ five customers. Andre Torres, an engineer for
                     (4. hold)

StarX, said, "Before, only astronauts could travel to space. Now, the sky is the

limit. Literally. Anyone can go." StarX is competing with other companies to

provide safe, affordable space travel.

Still, the public worries about safety. Torres said that safety is StarX's top

concern. "We _____ to all of the government's safety standards. In
                 (5. keep)

fact, in some cases, we exceed them," he said. "Plus, we have advanced

technology on the ground. If something happened in flight, we can

_____, using computer systems to make the necessary corrections
   (6. step in)

from Earth." Records for the company indicate zero accidents for three

_____ years.
(7. consecutive)

With twenty-five private space flights planned for next year, StarX is hoping

that the thrill of space travel will encourage people to fly with them.

Despite is a preposition that means "without being affected by the thing mentioned." That is, it is used to show that one thing happened or is true although something else might have prevented it.

The family had a great afternoon in the park **despite** *the cold weather.*

When the two things being contrasted are stated in separate sentences, *despite* may be used with the pronoun *this*.

A record number of people were hired this month. **Despite this,** *the tech department kept up with all employee computer needs.*

CORPUS

B. Fill in each blank with either *despite* or *despite this.*

1. Jonah completed the marathon ___*despite*___ the cramp in his left leg.

2. This weekend's rainstorm was the heaviest we've had in years. _____, we got through the storm with a dry basement!

3. _____ working a full day, I found the energy to get some weeding done in the garden.

Hence is an adverb that means "for this reason." In other words, it notes a cause-and-effect relationship between two things.

Today we're going to the beach, **hence** *the hat and towel.*
I've always loved taking things apart. **Hence,** *I decided to become an engineer.*

CORPUS

C. Complete each sentence with either *hence* or *despite this.*

1. Many satellites are built to work independently. ___*Hence*___, they can operate without human intervention.

2. Pilots work long hours during spaceflight. _____, they must be alert enough to perform difficult tasks.

3. Space shuttles burn a lot of fuel to leave Earth's gravity. _____, engineers are looking for ways to increase fuel economy.

About the Topic

A doctoral program is an advanced university-level program. Students can earn a degree called a PhD. Some engineering doctoral students study space debris. Space debris is scattered pieces of objects that circle Earth.

Before You Listen

Read these questions. Discuss your answers in a small group.

1. What do you think is a good reason to apply to a doctoral program?
2. Are you interested in traveling into space? Why or why not?
3. Do you think people will live on Mars one day? Explain.

Listen

Read the Listen for Main Ideas activity below. Go online to listen to a guest speaker address a group of students. The guest speaker talks about future jobs in space travel.

Listen for Main Ideas

Mark each sentence as *T* (true) or *F* (false). Work with a partner. Restate false sentences to make them correct.

_F_ 1. Dr. Karimi is giving a talk about government space flight organizations.
Dr. Karimi is talking about a private company.

___ 2. Dr. Holman was once an astronaut.

___ 3. Private space flight companies are as serious about safety as government space programs.

___ 4. People must have problem-solving skills if they want to work for a space program.

___ 5. There won't be many problems with traveling to or staying on Mars.

NOTE-TAKING SKILL   Annotating Lecture Notes

LEARN

When we annotate something, we add explanations and comments. Annotating your lecture notes helps you to think about the material. This helps you better understand and remember the information you hear in the lecture. As you write your notes, use symbols to quickly mark places you wish to add annotations. Leave space for annotations as well.

Here are some common annotation techniques:

- Underline terms you want to look up later.
- Place a star or other mark next to important points.
- Add notes for places to find more information about a topic.
- Write a question mark next to information you want to confirm or find later.
- Add any notes about points you remember from the lecture afterwards.

A. Listen to the first part of the lecture again. Look at the example of a student's annotated lecture notes. With a partner, discuss how notes made during the lecture compare to annotations the student added later.

- Science Day Discussion, May 4

  To work in space, study physics, engineering, math, ? ?
  · geology, biology

  Dr. Marwan Karimi, Asahi Space Systems, was a student here

  Requirements to be astronaut—good eyesight?
  · Bachelor's degree or higher, math, engineering, biology, physical science
  · eyesight

  Engineer, rocket specialist, education

  (Private) space travel companies <u>successors</u> to gov't
  How are private space companies funded?
  person (people?) or thing that comes after someone else

  Asahi Space Systems, other companies

  Non-astronauts still work with astronauts

APPLY

 A. Listen to the rest of the lecture. Continue to take notes on your own.

B. Annotate your notes. Underline two words you don't know, and look them up in your dictionary. Add the meanings to your notes. Compare your annotations with a partner.

 C. Now replay the audio. Compare your annotated notes against what Professor Holman and Dr. Karimi say about space science.

Vocabulary Activities

A. Complete the Word Form Chart with the correct form of the target words in the box below. Use a dictionary to check your answers.

allocate	classic	cooperate	cooperatively	revenue
allocated	classical	cooperation	differentiate	
allocation	classics	cooperative	differentiated	

Word Form Chart			
Noun	**Verb**	**Adjective**	**Adverb**
	allocate		

B. Read these excerpts from a lecture about engineering and Mars. For each sentence, circle the word or phrase in parentheses that has the same meaning as the underlined word in the sentence. Compare your answers with a partner.

1. For humans to live on Mars, many nations need to <u>cooperate</u> (*decide* / *work together* / *compete*) to bring resources to the "red planet."

2. Creating a dome for humans to live in is a <u>classic</u> (*traditional* / *new* / *overused*) solution for dealing with the thin atmosphere of Mars.

3. Scientists are using robots to <u>differentiate</u> (*make a list of* / *find new sources of* / *tell the difference between*) the elements found on Mars.

4. Private companies are <u>allocating</u> (*trading* / *distributing* / *looking for*) time and money to build shuttles that can carry people to Mars.

Cooperate is a verb that means "to work with someone else to achieve something" or "to be helpful by doing what someone asks you to do." Often, the word *cooperate* collocates with the preposition *with.*

> Our company is **cooperating with** a Mexican firm on a new project.
> NASA and the private companies will **cooperate with** each other to make sure the new shuttles are safe.

Cooperative is the adjective form of the word. The noun form is *cooperation*.

> Our ideal employee is efficient, communicative, and **cooperative**.
> We appreciated the designer's **cooperation** as we adapted her plans for the company logo.

CORPUS

C. Complete each sentence with the correct form of *cooperate*. Then discuss with a partner what it means to be a cooperative person.

1. Because of increased _cooperation_ on the International Space Station, a multi-country mission to Mars might be possible in the next 20 years.

2. Multiple countries have been _____ for many years on the International Space Station.

3. Successful astronauts must be patient, strong, and _____ .

4. Missions to Mars will be easier with the _____ of different space programs.

5. Asahi Space Systems has _____ with global partners to provide public space flights.

Straightforward is an adjective. It means "easy to do or understand" or "simple."

*Information presented in this text is **straightforward**, thorough, and well illustrated.*

When used to describe a person, *straightforward* means "honest and open."

*Marcel is **straightforward** in his answers.*

CORPUS

D. For each sample sentence on the left, list which meaning of *straightforward* is being used. Use one meaning twice.

_a_ 1. I appreciate straightforward answers to my questions about car insurance.

a. easy to do or understand

___ 2. The newly revised lab procedure was much more straightforward.

b. honest and open

___ 3. Kanna is sometimes a little too straightforward, so I don't think she'd make the best diplomat.

c. simple

___ 4. We took the most straightforward route through the woods.

About the Topic

The International Space Station (ISS) is a large satellite that orbits Earth. Astronauts from several countries live and do research on the ISS. Engineers are working to increase fuel economy, which is how far a vehicle can travel on a certain amount of fuel. This will make it cheaper to travel to space.

Before You Listen

Read these questions. Discuss your answers in a small group.

1. Press conferences are used to announce important news. Have you seen a press conference recently? If so, tell what it was about.

2. Do you think all nations should contribute to the International Space Station? Explain.

3. Imagine how space travel will change in the next 20 to 30 years. What do you think will be different in the future?

◀ Listen

Read the Listen for Main Ideas activity below. Go online to listen to a press conference. A space tourism company is giving information about its business plans.

◀ Listen for Main Ideas

Read the questions about the audio. Work with a partner to ask and answer these questions.

1. What is the purpose of the press conference?

2. What do the speakers say about fuel efficiency?

3. What differentiates the Asahi-Orion partnership from other space tourism operations?

PRESENTATION SKILL | Signaling the End of a Speech

LEARN

Using key words to signal the end of your speech will help the audience to anticipate and better understand your conclusion. A clear, strong finish gives your audience a lasting positive impression. For example, you can use the phrase *in summary* to let the audience know you are about to summarize key ideas from your speech. Similarly, you can introduce your conclusion with phrases such as *To wrap up, ...* or *Finally, ...*

You can also use signal phrases to "turn the floor over to," or introduce, a new speaker. In the press conference, Dr. Shinobara introduces his colleague by saying "I'm going to *turn the floor over to* Gloria to explain the nature of this cooperation."

Here are some signal phrases to use to signal the end of a speech:

Signal a conclusion	Give the floor to a new speaker
In conclusion, ...	Now I'll turn it over to ...
To conclude, ...	I'd like to introduce ... to talk about ...
Finally, ...	Up next, we have ...
I'll leave you with this ...	
Now I'd like to open it up for questions.	
Any questions?	

APPLY

A. Listen to the press conference again. Write key words the speaker uses to signal the end of a speech. Share your list with your partner and add any items that you may have missed.

_____

_____

_____

B. Discuss the following questions with a partner. Listen carefully to your partner's answers, so you can summarize them for the class.

1. Would you ever consider taking a commercial flight into space? Explain.

2. In your opinion, what is a reasonable price for a trip into space?

3. In the future, do you think commercial space flight will become a common alternative to airplane travel? Why or why not?

C. Summarize your partner's answers in a short speech. Present your summary to a small group or the class. Use key words to signal the end of your speech and to introduce the next speaker.

In conclusion, these are my partner's opinions about commercial space flight.
Up next, we have Janet, who will give you a summary of her partner's answers.

LEARN

Most two-syllable nouns, adjectives, and verbs have a predictable stress pattern. When a word, for example, *subject*, could be a noun, a verb, and an adjective, you usually differentiate the words by changing the word stress.

A. Go online to listen to the words in the chart. Notice that the nouns are stressed on the first syllable and verbs are stressed on the second syllable. Adjectives have a variable stress pattern.

Nouns	Verbs	Adjectives
abstract	————	abstract
complex	————	complex
content	content	content
converse	converse	converse
subject	subject	subject

B. Go online to listen to the shifting stress.

Nouns	Verbs	Nouns	Verbs
1. conduct	conduct	5. impact	impact
2. conflict	conflict	6. progress	progress
3. contract	contract	7. project	project
4. contrast	contrast	8. reject	reject

APPLY

A. Practice saying the words in Learn, activities A and B.

B. Go online to listen. Fill in the table with the words that you hear. Write the words in the correct box. Circle the syllable that has the stress. Compare answers with a partner.

	1	2	3	4
A				
B		con(duct)		
C				
D				

C. Work with a partner. Design a dictation chart like the one in activity B. Use these shifting nouns and verbs: *decrease, export, increase, object, permit, present, record.* Include both stress patterns in your table and circle the stressed syllables. Write only one word per box.

D. Join another pair. Take turns giving your dictations.
Speakers: Say the location of a word, pronounce it, and put it into a phrase or sentence.
Listeners: Write the words in the table on the right. Circle the stress. When you have completed the table, check your answers.

	1	2	3	4
A				
B				
C				
D				

C4 / increase / an increase in costs

E. Work in a small group. Choose a topic from the box. Start a conversation.

Tell us about ...	Tell us about a time when ...
a project you're working on	you made an impact on someone
how an increase in pay would change your life	you weren't permitted to do something
a contract you signed (or didn't sign)	your needs conflicted with someone else's
what you need in order to be content in life	you found it difficult to converse with someone
how your English is progressing	you objected to a decision

End of Unit Task

In this unit, you learned to annotate lecture notes and use signal phrases to signal the end of a speech. In this task, you will prepare a short speech and take notes during your group members' speeches.

A. Take this survey about your opinions toward funding space exploration.

	Strongly agree	Somewhat agree	Somewhat disagree	Strongly disagree
Exploring space has helped with many inventions.	◯	◯	◯	◯
We should spend money exploring Earth, not space.	◯	◯	◯	◯
Space exploration inspires humans to advance.	◯	◯	◯	◯
Spending billions on space travel is a waste of money.	◯	◯	◯	◯
Private companies can explore space better than governments.	◯	◯	◯	◯
Government funding is necessary because space exploration takes time and money.	◯	◯	◯	◯

B. Compare your survey results with a partner. Discuss any questions that you and your partner answered differently.

C. Complete the survey to make a short speech (one to two minutes) arguing for or against increased funding for space travel. Notice which survey questions you answered with "strongly agree" or "strongly disagree." Include these reasons in your speech or write your own.

Circle one: I am (for / against) increased government funding for space travel. Three reasons for my opinion are:

1. _____

2. _____

3. _____

D. Include two new words or phrases in your speech. Below are words you did not study in this unit. Look up the definitions in your dictionary and check with your instructor about how to use them. As your group members take notes, they will practice highlighting the new words they hear. After your speech, explain the new words and your group members can annotate their notes with the definition. Choose two words or phrases from the box below.

capacity	innovation	notable	public funding
frontier	inspire	oppose	support
funders	multinational	private funding	traverse

E. Choose phrases from the box on page 69 to signal the end of your speech and introduce the next speaker from your group.

F. Listen carefully and take notes while your group members give their speeches. Use your note-taking skills to annotate your notes. Remember to mark unknown vocabulary words you hear so you can annotate your notes with the definitions.

Self-Assessment		
Yes	**No**	
☐	☐	I successfully annotated my lecture notes with key ideas and new words.
☐	☐	I successfully used signal phrases to introduce a new speaker and / or indicate the end of a speech.
☐	☐	I correctly used stress on two-syllable words that have variable stress.
☐	☐	I can correctly use the target vocabulary words from the unit.

Discussion Questions

With a partner or in a small group, discuss the following questions.

1. What are the advantages of privatizing the space industry?

2. People worry that businesses care more about making money than safety. Do you think this is a risk with privatized space travel?

3. Do you think governments should continue to fund space research?

Our Amazing Brains

In this unit, you will

> learn about how the brain works.
> increase your understanding of the target academic words for this unit.

LISTENING AND SPEAKING SKILLS

> The Cornell Method to Take Notes
> Asking For and Giving Clarification
> **PRONUNCIATION** Reducing the *h* in *he*

Self-Assessment

Think about how well you know each target word, and check (✓) the appropriate column. I have…

TARGET WORDS	never seen this word before.	heard or seen the word but am not sure what it means.	heard or seen the word and understand what it means.	used the word confidently in *either* speaking or writing.
AWL				
🔑 adapt				
🔑 area				
clarify				
comprise				
🔑 create				
🔑 crucial				
🔑 dominate				
🔑 intense				
🔑 involve				
🔑 major				
perceive				
🔑 somewhat				
🔑 stress				
🔑 visual				

🔑 Oxford 3000™ keywords

Vocabulary Activities

Word Form Chart			
Noun	**Verb**	**Adjective**	**Adverb**
adaptation adaptability	adapt	adaptive	_____
creation creativity creator	create recreate	creative	creatively
involvement	involve	involved uninvolved	_____
perception	perceive	perceived	_____
stress	stressed	stressed stressful unstressed	_____

A. Using the target words in the Word Form Chart, complete the paragraph below. Be sure to use the correct form and tense of each word. Use the words in parentheses to help you.

Scientists once had the _perception_ that when people became adults and

(1. idea)

their bodies stopped growing, their brains stopped developing, too. Now

research shows that our brains can change throughout our lives. In fact,

our brains are always _____ to our behavior. If we feel constant

(2. adjusting)

_____, our brains will replace their neuron cells more slowly. On the

(3. pressure)

other hand, if we do things that make us feel calm, our brains _____

(4. produce)

new connections quickly. The parts of the brain that are _____

(5. used in)

concentration and _____ other people's feelings also become thicker.

(6. recognizing)

This means that we can actually become more _____ by doing

(7. inventive)

relaxing activities!

B. Some words have multiple meanings. For the target words below, match the dictionary definitions on the left with the example sentences on the right.

area (noun)

Definitions

b 1. part of a town, a country, or the world

___ 2. the size of a surface in mathematics

___ 3. a space used for a particular activity

___ 4. a particular part of a subject or activity

Example Sentences

a. There is a play area for children in our new apartment building.

b. Prices are expensive in the area around the university.

c. Her area of expertise is nueroscience.

d. To find the area of our classroom, we must multiply the length by the width.

stressed (adjective)

Definitions

___ 1. too anxious and tired to be able to relax

___ 2. pronounced with emphasis

___ 3. something that had a lot of physical pressure put on it

Example Sentences

a. Nouns and main verbs in a sentence are usually stressed.

b. The students felt stressed before the final exam.

c. Stressed concrete beams are often used in construction.

Dominant means "more important, powerful, or noticeable than other things." In biology, for example, a dominant gene determines eye color, hair color, and other physical attributes.

> *In humans, brown eyes are **dominant** over blue eyes.*

Other things can be referred to as *dominant*, such as a theme, a culture, or a role.

> *Power is a **dominant** theme in his writing.*

> *The **dominant** feature of the room was the bright red walls.*

CORPUS

C. Match each phrase with *dominant* to the correct example sentence.

c 1. dominant personality

___ 2. dominant gene

___ 3. dominant characteristic

a. Stone structures are a common feature of many ancient civilizations.

b. Tina and her daughter have brown eyes.

c. Joanne always takes control of the situation.

About the Topic

Neuroscience is the study of the brain and other neurons in the body. Neuroscientist Dr. John Medina wants to make discoveries in his field of study easy for all people to understand. He outlines the way our brains really work in his book, *Brain Rules.*

Before You Watch

Read these questions. Discuss your answers in a small group.

1. What is an I.Q. (intelligence quotient) score? Have you ever taken an I.Q. test?

2. Which sense do you think is stronger, sight or hearing? Give an example.

3. Memories are often tied to a specific smell. Is there a smell that reminds you of a past event?

Watch

Read the Listen for Main Ideas activity below. Go online to watch Dr. John Medina introduce his book, *Brain Rules.* Dr. Medina talks about some of the things we know and don't know about how our brains work.

Listen for Main Ideas

Mark each sentence as *T* (true) or *F* (false). Work with a partner. Restate false sentences to make them correct.

_T_ 1. Dr. Medina compares the number of neurons in our brains to stars in the galaxy.

___ 2. A person who is very good in math will have a high I.Q. score.

___ 3. The video gives examples of extraordinary things some people can do with their brains.

___ 4. Humans are not good about following the "Brain Rules" Dr. Medina covers in his book.

NOTE-TAKING SKILL The Cornell Method to Take Notes

LEARN

The Cornell Method is a way to take notes that involves dividing your paper into three sections. The three sections help you take notes in class, study what you wrote down, and remember what you heard. Read the instructions below.

1. Divide your paper into three sections and label A, B, and C. (See Figure 1.)

2. Listen and take notes in Section B. Don't write anything in Sections A or C.

3. Compare your notes with a partner. Add information you missed to Section B.

4. Listen again. Add details, examples, and missing information to Section B.

Figure 1

5. When you finish listening, write questions in Section A about the information in Section B. These will help you study later.

6. In Section C, write a summary of your notes from Section B.

Section A	Section B
· What do we know about the human brain?	· little known about the brain
	· brain: fast, clever, adaptive
· Why did the author create Brain Rules?	· Author's goal = introduce 12 brain rules.
· What are some topics that Brain Rules covers?	· Topics:
	exercise
	memory
· _____	stress
	sleep
	_____
	· We ignore brain rules
	Examples:
	1. Impossible to drive and _____ at the same time
	2. _____ .

1. Take notes in Section B while you listen. Compare your notes with a partner. Then add information.

2. Write questions in Section A about the notes you took in Section B.

Section C

3. Write a summary of your notes from Section B in Section C.

APPLY

A. Watch the video again and complete Section B above.

B. Compare your answers with a partner. Add any information you think is important.

C. Write a question in Section A for each point in Section B. Work with a partner. Ask and answer each other's questions. Confirm or correct the information in Section B.

D. As a class, write a summary of the video in Section C.

Vocabulary Activities

Word Form Chart

Noun	Verb	Adjective	Adverb
clarification	clarify	clarified	_____
_____	_____	crucial	crucially
intensity intenseness	intensify	intensified intense	intensely
visualization	visualize	visual	visually

A. Complete the paragraph below using the correct form of the words in the Word Form Chart. Use the words in parentheses to help you.

Advertisers know that memories and emotions are ___*crucial*___ to a person's
                                                   (1. important)

decisions. In a type of research called "neuromarketing," some companies

measure people's brain activity to learn which features of an advertisement,

such as a _____ reminder of a fun childhood moment, send
            (2. seen)

messages directly to the part of the brain that holds emotional memories.

Neuromarketing shows that creating _____ emotional reaction
                                    (3. a strong)

is a good way to convince people to buy products. Companies that use

neuromarketing _____, however, that advertisements are unable to
                (4. explain)

actually control shopper's decisions.

B. Cross out the word or phrase in parentheses with a different meaning from the others. Use a dictionary as needed. Compare answers with a partner.

1. Acceptance into engineering school is very difficult. Applicants must participate in (*an intense / a demanding / an involved*) series of tests to be accepted.

2. People can lower the pain they feel from an injury through (*visualizing / picturing / listening to / imagining*) a beautiful place.

3. To (*adapt / clarify / explain / define*) the effect brain-training games have on the mind, scientists studied people as they played these games for several hours a day.

4. Different skills are connected with different sides of the brain. If your left side of the brain is (*crucial / stressed / dominant / commanding*), you may be better at logic games.

The verb *comprise* means "to be made up of something" or "to include."

*The collection **comprises** 426 books.*

Comprise is often used in the passive voice with *of*.

Notice that:

<u>*(The whole)*</u> is comprised of <u>*(parts)*</u>.

*Our final grade is **comprised of** two test scores, ten quizzes, and class participation.*

CORPUS

C. Work with a partner. Read each incomplete sentence and identify the "whole" and the "parts" of the topic. Complete the sentences. Some sentences require the word *comprise* by itself, while other sentences require the passive collocation *to be comprised of*. Be sure to use the correct form and tense of *comprise* and *to be*.

1. Dr. Medina's book about the brain _____*comprises*_____ twelve rules.

2. Early humans' daily activities _____ of walking, eating, and sleeping.

3. The human brain _____ four lobes.

4. My weekend plans _____ of seeing friends, doing laundry, and reading.

5. Some advanced medications _____ of plants found in nature.

About the Topic

When you study with a group of students, you can discuss what you learned in class, review your notes, and confirm that you understood what the professor said. These discussions, and explaining class material to other students, can also help you understand and remember the class material better.

Before You Listen

Discuss these questions with a partner.

1. Have you ever played "brain games," such as crossword puzzles, sudoku, or memory games?

2. Do you think "brain games" can make you smarter? Why or why not?

3. In your opinion, what are some good ways for people to keep their minds active?

Listen

Read the Listen for Main Ideas activity below. Go online to listen to three students in a study session. They are preparing for an exam in their neuroscience class. Listen to them review their lecture notes.

Listen for Main Ideas

Work with a partner. Answer the questions about the study session.

1. Did the students enjoy the lecture yesterday?

2. What are the two main areas discussed related to brain development?

3. Do all kinds of exercise have the same benefit for the brain?

4. Does the professor think that brain games are helpful?

SPEAKING SKILL Asking For and Giving Clarification

LEARN

Study sessions provide you with a chance to ask your classmates for clarification on any point you didn't understand.

When you don't understand something, whether in class or elsewhere, you can ask for clarification by using the questions and phrases from the chart in the left column. When you are explaining or giving clarification, use the phrases from the chart in the right column.

Asking for clarification	Giving clarification
Did you understand the part about … ?	I think he meant that …
What did he mean when he said … ?	The way I understand it is …
Could you give me an example … ?	To give you an example …
What was he saying about … ?	I wrote down that …

A. Listen to the review session again. Write down the clarification phrases you hear in the chart below.

Asking for clarification	Giving clarification

B. Compare your phrases with a partner. Add any phrases you missed.

C. In groups of three, choose a role for each person for the discussion below (Professor, Student A, or Student B). Together, complete the dialogue aloud. Choose the phrases from the list on page 80 that best complete the discussion.

Professor: Dr. Medina suggests that we might be more productive at work or in class if we were more physically active.

Student A: _____ ?

Professor: Sure. One example he gives is for people to walk on a treadmill, rather than sit in a chair, when they're working at their computers.

Student B: Professor, _____
that people don't pay attention to boring things?

Professor: _____
That's why he tries to tell stories or give examples so that students don't get bored.

Student A: _____
the importance of sleep? I wasn't sure what was meant by "the brain processes what was learned during the day."

Student B: _____
that while we sleep, our brain is reviewing everything that we learned that day.

D. Work in a small group. Choose one student to present a theory about the best way to learn. As a group, discuss what the speaker said. Ask each other for clarification. Then confirm your understanding with the speaker. Have each student present a theory.

LEARN

When you say the pronoun *he* in the middle of a sentence, the *h* disappears. Instead, you say a very quiet *e* sound and link it to the word before it. This makes *he* very hard to hear.

A. Go online to listen. Notice what happens to *he* and the word before it when *he* is in the middle of the sentence.

"wuzzy"

1. What was ̶h̶e saying about that?

"wuddy"

2. I can't remember what ̶h̶e was saying about that.

B. Go online to listen. Notice how we say the *h* when *he* begins a sentence or comes after a pause.

1. <u>He</u> said that exercise increases our oxygen flow.
2. For example, <u>he</u> said exercise helps our brains solve problems.

APPLY

A. Cross out the *h* in ̶h̶e and show the link with the word before it.

1. I think ̶h̶e meant …
2. I think he was …
3. I know he meant …
4. I know he said …
5. I thought he said …
6. I thought he meant …

B. Go online to listen. Repeat the phrases from Apply, activity A. Focus on the reduction, and make a smooth word connection.

Example: think | think ̶h̶e | think ̶h̶e meant | I think ̶h̶e meant …

C. Work with a partner. Use the phrases from Apply, activity A to have short dialogues.

A: I think he meant he would meet us after class …

B: I know he said "after class," but I thought he meant later this evening.

A: Oh, is that what you thought he meant?

B: Well, let's call him to find out what he meant for sure.

End of Unit Task

In this unit, you learned how to take notes using the Cornell Method, and how to ask for and give clarification in group study sessions. Review these skills by taking notes on a new video. As you review, ask for clarification from your classmates.

A. Go online to watch a video about a study that tested whether brain games make us smarter. Use the Cornell Method to take notes in Section B.

Section A	Section B
	• *The games invented tested: problem-solving, memory, math*
	• *Point of the study was* _____
	• _____
	• _____
	• _____
	• _____

Section C

This study was devised to answer the question: _____

B. Compare your notes with three other students. Ask for and give clarification using the phrases you wrote in Section B. Add any new or corrected information to Section B.

C. Watch again. Add details, examples, and missing information to Section B.

Asking for clarification	Giving clarification
Did you understand the part about … ?	I think he meant that …
What did he mean when he said … ?	The way I understand it is …
Could you give me an example … ?	To give you an example …
What was he saying about … ?	I wrote down that …

D. With your partner, create study questions about the information you wrote in Section B. Write these questions in Section A.

E. With your partner, write a summary of your notes in Section C.

F. Cover your answers. With your partner, ask and answer the questions you wrote in Section A.

Self-Assessment		
Yes	**No**	
☐	☐	I can use the Cornell Method to take notes.
☐	☐	I asked for clarification for the points I was not sure about.
☐	☐	I was able to clarify some points for my classmate.
☐	☐	I can reduce h when it appears in the middle of a sentence.
☐	☐	I can correctly use the target vocabulary from the unit.

Discussion Questions

With a partner or in a small group, discuss the following questions.

1. How can intelligence be measured?
2. Why does our brain produce illusions?
3. Do you think brain games are worthwhile?

Dangerous Gossip?

In this unit, you will
> learn about the psychology of gossip.
> increase your understanding of the target academic words for this unit.

LISTENING AND SPEAKING SKILLS
> Listening for Fact and Opinion
> Citing Information
> **PRONUNCIATION** Reducing Phrasal Modals

Self-Assessment
Think about how well you know each target word, and check (✓) the appropriate column. I have…

TARGET WORDS	never seen this word before.	heard or seen the word but am not sure what it means.	heard or seen the word and understand what it means.	used the word confidently in *either* speaking or writing.
AWL				
attribute				
🔑 exclude				
gender				
🔑 imply				
initiate				
🔑 license				
🔑 philosophy				
🔑 register				
🔑 relevant				
statistic				
🔑 tape				
🔑 theory				
🔑 ultimate				
🔑 valid				

🔑 Oxford 3000™ keywords

85

Vocabulary Activities

Noun	Verb	Adjective	Adverb
attribution	attribute	attributable	_____
exclusion	exclude	exclusive	exclusively
gender	_____	_____	_____
_____	imply	implied	_____
license	license	licensed	_____
register	register	registered	_____
tape	tape	taped	_____
validation	invalidate	invalid, valid	validly

A. Complete the paragraph below with the correct form of a target word from the Word Form Chart. Use the words in parentheses to help you.

Some psychologists say things that ___*imply*___ that gossip is useful. It can
              (1. suggest)

help people learn good behavior, they say. But everyone knows gossip can

also be harmful. In one study, people were given _____ messages
                                                  (2. recorded)

with positive or negative gossip. Psychologists asked the people to listen and

assume the things they heard were said about them. Sixty-eight percent of

people who heard the positive comments _____ higher self-esteem.
                                          (3. expressed)

However, 96 percent of people who listened to the negative comments

reported lower self-esteem. Psychologists believe that low self-esteem can

be _____ to negative gossip. They have found this is true in people
    (4. connected to)

of either _____ . Science suggests that gossip has a _____
          (5. male or female)   (6. justifiable)

place in society. But that does not give us _____ to gossip carelessly.
                                             (7. permission)

Negative gossip _____ people from groups and makes them feel bad
                 (8. leaves out)

about themselves.

The word *valid* is an adjective. It means "legally or officially acceptable," "based on what is logical or true." The opposite of *valid* is *invalid*.

> Gossip sometimes provides **valid** information about a person's behavior.

> Maria's finish time was declared **invalid** because she missed some checkpoints during the race.

The verb form, *validate*, means "to prove that something is true" or "to officially state that something is useful or acceptable." The noun form is *validity*.

> I always ask for my employment contracts because promises made over the phone are difficult to **validate**.

> The scientist doubted the **validity** of the research study.

CORPUS

B. Which of the following are valid or invalid things to consider when you are looking for a new apartment? Write *V* (valid) or *I* (invalid). Discuss your answers with a partner.

_V_ 1. The apartment has no smoke detector.

___ 2. Your potential neighbors are noisy.

___ 3. Your parents live nearby.

___ 4. The apartment hasn't been recently painted.

___ 5. The rent is too high.

___ 6. There are too many trees near the apartment.

___ 7. The landlord is a family friend.

___ 8. It is near good restaurants.

C. Read the sentences. Write the correct part of speech for the bold word in each sentence.

1. Researchers **invalidated** the results because the study was too small.
   _____verb_____

2. A research study has **validity** when its conclusion clearly relates to the real world. _____

3. Gossip can **exclude** people from certain groups. _____

4. Gossip is not **exclusive** to women. Men gossip just as much. _____

5. Many psychologists find gossip a **valid** phenomenon to study. _____

6. Psychologists find that while gossip can lead to **exclusion**, it can also bring groups of people closer together. _____

About the Topic

Psychology is the scientific study of the human mind. Psychologists particularly pay attention to human behaviors, such as gossiping. Gossip is informal talk about other people. The word *gossip* is often used negatively. But psychologists have learned that gossiping also has positive effects for individuals and society.

Before You Listen

Read these questions. Discuss your answers in a small group.

1. How might gossip have a positive effect?
2. When you overhear a conversation you aren't a part of, how do you feel afterward?
3. What experience have you had with gossip?

Listen

Read the Listen for Main Ideas activity below. Go online to listen to the first part of a lecture. The lecturer tells a story to introduce her talk about gossip and group behavior.

Listen for Main Ideas

Mark each sentence as *T* (true) or *F* (false). Work with a partner. Restate false sentences to make them correct.

_F_ 1. The speaker talks about why gossip is harmful. *The speaker talks about how gossip is helpful.*

___ 2. Nadia used to take long breaks without telling her manager.

___ 3. The man gossiped because he doesn't like Nadia.

___ 4. Gossiping is not a common behavior.

___ 5. We can learn useful information from people who gossip.

LEARN

Speakers often share both facts and opinions. They frequently support statements of fact with examples or data. Listen for names, dates, places, or events to identify facts in a speech.

Opinions, on the other hand, may be more difficult to recognize. An opinion is something a person thinks or believes. Opinions may or may not be based on facts. Words that express informal judgment in some way usually indicate an opinion. Look at the following list for examples:

bad	better	less	nice	terrible
believe	feel	most	seem	think
best	good	must	should	worst

For example, the guest lecturer says gossip is her favorite topic because "**most** people don't understand what it's really about." She also says that many people think that "only people with **bad** manners gossip." These are clear examples of opinions. Opinions often include judgment words.

In contrast, the speaker includes several facts in her guest lecture. For example, "I'm an assistant professor of psychology," and "Ordering was taking a long time, so I had to wait in line longer than usual." Facts often include the verb *be* and usually do not include judgment words.

APPLY

A. Take turns with a partner reading the following sentences aloud. Decide whether each sentence gives a fact (*F*) or an opinion (*O*).

_O_ 1. I believe that social media can be addicting.

___ 2. There are more than one billion people using social media in the world.

___ 3. The fastest growing group of social media users is people aged 45–54.

___ 4. The most useful social media site for job-hunting is LinkedIn.

___ 5. More than half of people who use social media use a mobile device.

___ 6. Young people shouldn't use social media until they are at least 16.

B. Think of three more statements about social media or gossip. Take turns with a partner sharing your statements. Decide whether the other person's statements are fact or opinion. Explain.

 C. Listen to the audio about gossip again. Write down two opinions that you hear. Which word in the sentence lets you know it is an opinion? Share your answers with a partner.

D. Go online to listen to a clip from the audio. List at least three facts and three opinions that you hear. Compare your list with a partner.

A. Put each word in the box in the correct column, based on the target word for which it is a synonym. Use your dictionary to check the meaning of new words.

concluding	fact	information	linked	pertinent
connected	figure	key	number	related
establish	final	launch	optimum	set up

initiate	relevant	statistic	ultimate
_____	_____	_____	_concluding_
_____	_____	_____	_____
_____	_____	_____	_____
_____	_____	_____	_____

A *theory* is "an idea or set of ideas that is intended to explain something." In science, a *theory* is specifically a statement that summarizes many studies and a large amount of evidence.

*New information and facts test the truth of established **theories**.*

Informally, a *theory* can also refer to "an idea that someone believes is true but that is not proved."

*Casey has a **theory** about how our favorite TV program will end, but he won't share it with us.*

As an academic discipline, *philosophy* is "the study of ideas and beliefs." A *philosophy* is also "a belief or set of beliefs that gives rules about how to behave, or tries to explain the meaning of life."

*A new professor in the **philosophy** department specializes in studying ethics in science.*

*Neil's **philosophy** is that it's better to take your time and get a job done right the first time.*

 CORPUS

B. Decide whether each item is a *philosophy* or a *theory*. Write P (philosophy) or T (theory) next to each item. Discuss your reasons with a partner.

_P_ 1. start the day with a healthy breakfast

____ 2. nature positively affects people's moods

____ 3. there are other planets that can support life

____ 4. babies learn social behavior by watching other people

____ 5. always arrive early

Word Form Chart			
Noun	**Verb**	**Adjective**	**Adverb**
initiative initiation	initiate	initiated	_____
relevance irrelevance	_____	relevant irrelevant	_____

C. Fill in each blank with the correct form of a target word from the Word Form Chart. Use your dictionary as needed. Compare answers with a partner.

1. All the sentences in a paragraph should be about the same topic. When I edit my writing, I look for _irrelevant_ information to delete.

2. Employers want employees who are self-starters. They are looking for people who have _____ and don't need to be told what to do next.

3. The volunteer group has a dinner every year to _____ new members into the group. They give them uniforms and welcome them as official members.

4. Some math students complain that they have to take classes in history or language arts. They don't see the _____ of these classes to their future careers.

5. When you talk about your interests on a job application, you should include only ones that are _____ to the position.

6. When the project was _____, people had many doubts. Now they are very excited about the new building.

Ultimate means "being or happening at the end," or "last or final." It is also used to describe the greatest or most extreme example of something. In this meaning, it is also used as a noun.

> Her **ultimate** goal is to get a job in financial management.

> This resort is the **ultimate** in relaxation and comfort.

CORPUS

D. What might be the *ultimate* goal for people in each of the following professions? Make a list. Discuss your answers in a small group.

1. a writer: _to write a book, to publish a book_

2. an engineer: _____

3. a surgeon: _____

4. an actor: _____

5. an architect: _____

6. a parent: _____

7. a painter: _____

8. a scientist: _____

9. an athlete: _____

About the Topic

A reputation is an opinion. It is the opinion that people in general have about what someone is like. Reputations are generally formed through gossip.

Before You Listen

Read these questions. Discuss your answers in a small group.

1. Do you think managers consider a person's reputation when they hire? Why or why not?

2. Do people's reputations factor into your interest in being friends with them? Explain.

3. When would you look at reviews before purchasing a product?

Listen

Read the Listen for Main Ideas activity below.
Go online to listen to the second half of the lecture.
The lecturer continues a discussion about the
importance of gossip.

Listen for Main Ideas

Read the questions about the audio. Work with a partner to ask and answer these questions.

1. What is the key reason gossip is important?

2. How is a reputation important?

3. Can one piece of gossip change a person's opinion of someone else?

4. How can gossip benefit people?

PRESENTATION SKILL   Citing Information

LEARN

When you give a speech or a presentation, you often need to cite information from something you have heard or read. It is called plagiarism if a person presents someone else's work or ideas as his / her own. When you discuss other people's ideas, you need to give them credit in order to avoid plagiarism. This is especially important if you are directly quoting another person word for word.

Sometimes you may need to directly quote someone else in a presentation. For a direct quote, place the author's exact words in quotation marks.

According to Professor Smith, gossip is "how groups teach rules of behavior to new members."

Other times it may be more useful to paraphrase an author's ideas. To avoid plagiarism, you still need to credit the person even though you are putting the ideas in your own words.

Professor Smith's work indicates that gossip helps new group members learn a group's expected rules of behavior.

Phrases that indicate direct quotes	Phrases that show paraphrasing
According to (author), " ... "	In a study of (topic), (author) found that ...
As (author) said, " ... "	A study by (author) shows that ...
To quote (author), " ... "	The work of (author) indicates that ...
(Author) found that " ... "	(Author) concludes that ...
	Research by (author) suggests that ...

APPLY

A. Work with a partner. For each item, combine the information into a quote or paraphrase.

1. Dr. Flores and Dr. Haviland / gossip can make people feel more connected to their close friends

   The work of Dr. Flores and Dr. Haviland indicates that gossip can make people feel more connected to their close friends.

   According to Dr. Flores and Dr. Haviland, "gossip can make people feel more connected to their close friends."

2. Kenneth Mitchell / some teenagers reported feeling very unhappy after using social media for several hours

3. Patricia Acs / gossiping about celebrities is a way to see if someone shares your interests

4. Researchers at the Morita Institute / people were more likely to believe information in gossip magazines than events they saw with their own eyes

5. Psychologist Richard Wood / people bond over negative gossip, especially about sports and work

B. Go online to listen to three audio clips from the guest lecturer. Write the citations you hear. Compare your list with a partner.

_____

_____

_____

_____

C. Work with a partner to write a few interview questions about gossip. Use your questions to interview three classmates. Practice quoting or paraphrasing their responses to your partner.

LEARN

Phrasal modals are made up of two or more words—usually a verb or a modal, plus the word *to*. Most English speakers reduce phrasal modals in both formal and informal speech.

A. Look at the chart. Then go online to listen to reduced phrasal modals in everyday conversation.

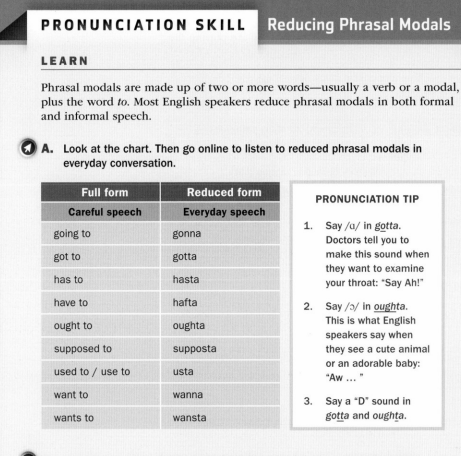

Full form	Reduced form
Careful speech	Everyday speech
going to	gonna
got to	gotta
has to	hasta
have to	hafta
ought to	oughta
supposed to	supposta
used to / use to	usta
want to	wanna
wants to	wansta

PRONUNCIATION TIP

1. Say /ɑ/ in *go**tt**a*. Doctors tell you to make this sound when they want to examine your throat: "Say Ah!"

2. Say /ɔ/ in *ough**t**a*. This is what English speakers say when they see a cute animal or an adorable baby: "Aw ... "

3. Say a "D" sound in *go**tt**a* and *ough**t**a*.

B. Go online to listen to two students gossiping. Pay close attention to the reduced forms.

APPLY

A. Go online to listen to the students again. Write their conversation. Use the full forms of the verbs. You may need to listen a few times. Check your conversation with a partner.

B. Look at your conversation from Apply, activity A. Write the reduced verb forms above the full forms.

gonna
You're not going to believe what happened to John!

C. Go online to listen to the conversation again and follow along with your notes. Shadow the speakers by speaking at the same time and match their speed, stress, rhythm, and intonation. Pay close attention to the reduced forms.

D. Practice the conversation with a partner.

E. Work in a small group. Ask and answer questions using reduced phrasal modals.

Q: *What's something you'd like to learn to do? What steps would you hafta take in order to do it?*

A: *I'd like to learn to play the piano, but I'd hafta find the time, money, and energy to take lessons.*

Questions	Answers
What are you going to do this weekend?	I'm going to ...
What is something you have to do by the end of the month?	I've got to ...
What is one thing you want to accomplish in the next five years?	I want to ...
In your culture, what are you supposed to do when you sneeze?	You're supposed to ...
What is one way you have changed over time?	I used to ... / I didn't use to ...

End of Unit Task

In this unit, you learned to listen for facts and opinion and to cite information in a presentation. You will practice both skills as you listen to two persuasive speeches and prepare a summary.

A. Work with a partner. Decide who will listen for facts and who will listen for opinions. NOTE: For now, ignore the research citations that the students give. You will listen for those later.

B. Go online to listen to the persuasive statements. Take notes in the chart below. You may need to listen a few times to complete your notes.

Facts	Opinions

C. Compare your answers with another pair of students. Fill in any information you missed.

D. Listen again to the persuasive statements. This time, complete the citations. Compare your answers in the same group of four.

> According to research by Dr. Anna Lin, *the number of hours of sunshine* in a day has a direct relationship to how happy someone feels. She studied participants' moods over _____. To quote Dr. Lin, "People who lived in sunnier climates reported feeling happier overall."
>
> The work of another author, Sam Dubois, _____ rain actually does depress mood. _____, high humidity, or rain, is linked to a lack of energy and a lack of affection.
>
> In a study of _____, Dr. Jan Kemp from Humboldt University in Germany studied more than a thousand participants and found _____ between their moods and the weather.

E. Prepare a short summary of the audio. Explain each student's opinion and give two facts that support that opinion. Use at least one citation to support each student's argument.

F. Change the quoting and paraphrasing language for each citation. Review and use the phrases that indicate direct quotes and paraphrasing on page 93.

> *For example, if the audio said "According to research by Dr. Anna Lin ... " you can change it to "Dr. Anna Lin found that ... ."*

G. Present your summary in a small group. Remember to pay attention to your pronunciation.

Self-Assessment		
Yes	**No**	
☐	☐	I successfully listened for fact and opinion.
☐	☐	I correctly identified words that indicate an opinion.
☐	☐	I successfully used academic language to cite information.
☐	☐	I successfully summarized facts and opinions in a persuasive speech.
☐	☐	I practiced reducing modals as I spoke.
☐	☐	I can correctly use the target vocabulary words from the unit.

Discussion Questions

With a partner or in a small group, discuss the following questions.

1. Is gossip ever healthy?
2. Why is it important to cite sources when giving information?
3. If you state something but don't give sources, does that make it gossip?

9

Franchise Fun

In this unit, you will

> learn about franchise businesses.
> increase your understanding of the target academic words for this unit.

LISTENING AND SPEAKING SKILLS

> Recognizing Persuasive Speech
> Facilitating a Group Discussion
> **PRONUNCIATION** Linking

Self-Assessment

Think about how well you know each target word, and check (✓) the appropriate column. I have…

TARGET WORDS	never seen this word before.	heard or seen the word but am not sure what it means.	heard or seen the word and understand what it means.	used the word confidently in *either* speaking or writing.
AWL				
🔑 acquire				
🔑 adequate				
🔑 collapse				
🔑 ethnic				
🔑 grant				
🔑 nuclear				
precede				
🔑 publication				
rational				
regime				
restrain				
🔑 reverse				
🔑 route				
🔑 sum				

🔑 Oxford 3000™ keywords

Vocabulary Activities

A. Match the words in the box with their antonyms. Put each antonym into the correct column. Use your dictionary as needed. Compare your results with a partner.

come after	give up	lose	succeed
follow	hand over	nonsensical	trail
get rid of	llogical	senseless	unreasonable

acquire	precede	rational
lose	_____	_____
_____	_____	_____
_____	_____	_____
_____	_____	_____

Word Form Chart		
Noun	**Verb**	**Adjective**
restraint	restrain	restrained unrestrained
reverse reversal	reverse	reverse reversible irreversible
sum	sum	_____

B. Using the target words in the Word Form Chart, complete the paragraph below. Be sure to use the correct form and tense of each word.

It is difficult to run a business. First, business owners need to get all the right permits, or official documents. Then they need customers in order to stay in business. If customers aren't coming into the store or buying services, it is difficult to ___reverse___ that trend. Some businesses turn to advertising to
 (1. turn back)
attract customers. But advertising is expensive. Business owners have to be careful and show _____ when buying advertisements. _____
 (2. control)   (3. Unrestricted)
purchasing of advertisements can hurt profits. And with profits and expenses

comes the next challenge, managing a budget. A budget is a plan for how to spend money. Business owners need to add up all their expenses and income. If the _____ is inaccurate, business owners will have difficulty
(4. amount)
managing their budgets. Last, business owners have to follow a lot of rules. For example, a business has to meet cleanliness and safety standards. Customers like businesses that have a reputation for being clean and safe. But that reputation is _____ if standards are not maintained. To sum up, it
(5. changeable)
is not easy to run a business.

C. Work with a partner to complete the following sentences. Then share your answers with another group.

1. My exercise regime consists of _doing push-ups, running, and lifting weights_ .

2. Strict diet regimes for people who want to lose weight may include
_____ .

3. My study regime consists of _____ .

4. A training regime for a new job should include _____ .

D. With a partner, decide what might precede the following activities. Share your answers with another group.

1. Getting an "A" in a class: _studying hard, reviewing notes, and reading the textbook_

2. Running in a marathon: _____

3. Owning a business: _____

4. Going abroad on vacation: _____

5. Winning a photography contest: _____

6. Becoming fluent in English: _____

About the Topic

Some businesses become so popular that the owner wants to open new locations in other areas. These new locations, called *franchises*, are often owned by different people but they have the same name and services as the original business. Franchise owners pay a fee to the business owner for the right to use the company's brand name.

Before You Listen

Read these questions. Discuss your answers in a small group.

1. What are the most popular businesses where you live?
2. What do you know about owning a business?
3. What challenges do you think business owners face every day?

Listen

Read the Listen for Main Ideas activity below. Go online to listen to a man using persuasive speech to explain how he can help you run a successful franchise.

Listen for Main Ideas

Read the questions about the speech. Work with a partner to ask and answer these questions.

1. What is one advantage of opening a franchise?
2. What are two of the questions you should ask before opening a business?
3. How does competition affect business?

LISTENING SKILL   Recognizing Persuasive Speech

LEARN

People use lectures and presentations to make a point. They often try to persuade you to see their opinion or to take action. They sometimes do this by using facts. However, if you listen carefully, you can hear their opinions as well.

1. Use your prior knowledge about the topic and the speaker to understand the speaker's point of view. Ask yourself:

   Does this person have a strong opinion about a cause?

   Does this person make money by selling something?

   How could my opinion or action benefit this person?

2. Listen for clues about the speaker's opinion.

   It's a great idea ...

   I think you should ...

   This is a wonderful opportunity ...

   The worst option is ...

3. Focus on words used to describe the topic. Are these words positive or negative?

It would be beneficial to you …

They're easy to run …

You don't want … to happen to you …

4. If a speaker is trying to persuade you that taking an action will benefit you, he / she will personalize the language to you and use your name.

(*Name*), you should …

(*Name*), I know what you need.

You will definitely want to …

5. Listen for rhetorical questions, that is, questions that don't require a response, or that the speaker answers. This makes it seem like you agree with the speaker.

Do you think prices are too high? Sure you do. We all do.

It's what we all want, right?

Isn't it a great price?

How do we know? Because …

A. Read the following sentences from the presentation about franchises. Circle words that are generally positive and underline words that are generally negative.

1. Franchises are a great idea if you want to run your own business but are concerned about starting one yourself.

2. They're easy to run.

3. If you see increasing debt and decreasing sales, that might be a business you want to avoid.

4. These other franchise owners can help you develop and follow a regime that'll make your business as successful as their businesses.

B. Go online to listen to the presentation again. What persuasive language can you identify? Compare answers with a partner.

APPLY

A. Look at the sentences below. What does the person want you to do? How do you know? Discuss your answers with your partner.

1. This is the best car on the market for a young professional because it's affordable and stylish.

2. Nine out of ten dentists believe that flossing is more important than brushing your teeth.

3. It is dangerous to assume that you can pass a test without studying.

B. Go online to listen to a woman's advice about buying a franchise. What persuasive speech does she use? What does she want you to believe or do? Discuss with your partner.

Vocabulary Activities

Word Form Chart			
Noun	**Verb**	**Adjective**	**Adverb**
adequacy inadequacy	_____	adequate inadequate	adequately inadequately
collapse	collapse	collapsible	_____
ethnicity	_____	ethnic	_____

A. Fill in each blank with the appropriate word from the Word Form Chart. Use your dictionary as needed. Compare answers with a partner.

1. A sum of $50,000 is __inadequate__ to start a business. Most people need at least $250,000.

2. Future tablet computers will have _____ screens, so they can be folded to fit into pockets.

3. After the _____ of the Aria Bridge, people had to cross Palomar Bridge to get into town.

4. Several investors questioned the _____ of the company's business plan.

5. Some college applications ask students to state their _____. The question is usually optional.

6. The salesperson _____ quoted the cost of advertisements. They cost much more than he said.

7. A new business will _____ if it does not attract enough customers.

8. _____ food is popular in New York City.

B. Collocations are words that often go together. For example, *group* is often used with *ethnic*, as in *ethnic group*. Create collocations with the target words from this unit. Use a dictionary if necessary.

1. attack / disaster / energy / power / war / waste _____ *nuclear* _____

2. compensation / funding / information / preparation / water _____

3. financial / imminent / sudden / system / total _____

4. annual / monthly / new / stop / trade _____

Word Form Chart		
Noun	**Verb**	**Adjective**
grant	grant	_____
publication	_____	_____
route	route	routing

C. Using the target words in the Word Form Chart, complete the paragraph below. Be sure to use the correct form and tense of each word.

The traditional ___route___ for people to open a business is to invest large
(1. way)

sums of money in an idea. But some business ideas require more knowledge

than money. _____ such as *Smart Business* and *Technology Today*
(2. magazines)

have articles about such businesses. *Technology Today* wrote about Yousef

Al Massri's story. He noticed that the office staff had trouble working

with patients' paper medical records. So he wrote a program to put

patients' information onto the computer. Then he received a government

_____ to create a similar program for other hospitals. Now, hospitals
(3. award)

are _____ patients' information through a computerized database.
(4. sending)

When patients move, their medical records move with them. Yousef

built a successful company and wrote about his experience in a business

_____ .
(5. journal)

D. Work with a partner. Match the beginnings of the sentences on the left with the endings on the right to make complete sentences. Take turns saying the completed sentences.

_b_ 1. Applicants must route all employment questions

    2. When hiking, stick to the marked routes

    3. Studying every day is the route

    4. The airline rerouted the flight

a. because they are easier to walk on.

b. through Human Resources.

c. to Rome through Frankfurt.

d. to success with English.

About the Topic

On many radio stations, talk show hosts have to facilitate, or direct, roundtable discussions. Roundtable discussions are conversations where several people are talking. The hosts make sure the participants respond to each other's comments and answer questions. A facilitator's job is to keep the discussion on topic.

Before You Watch
Discuss these questions with a small group.

1. Imagine you are going start your own business. What kind of business would you open? Why?

2. What kind of personal traits do you need to be successful in business?

3. Would you prefer to work for yourself or someone else? Why?

Watch

Read the Listen for Main Ideas activity below. Go online to watch a roundtable discussion with several franchise owners.

Listen for Main Ideas
Read the questions about the video. Work with a partner to ask and answer these questions.

1. How would you describe the franchises discussed by their owners?

2. Two of the franchise owners have very different experiences with regard to receiving money to start a business. What were their experiences?

3. What are some challenges the franchise owners faced?

SPEAKING SKILL | Facilitating a Group Discussion

LEARN

Sometimes students work in groups in class. Groups work better when there is someone to facilitate the discussion. This person is called a *facilitator*. Their job is to keep the discussion focused on the topic and make sure everyone has a chance to contribute to the discussion. For example, he / she may politely interrupt someone who is speaking too much, or encourage a quieter speaker to join. The facilitator may also keep the discussion going when there is a pause by asking for opinions.

Here are some helpful phrases for facilitating a discussion:

Ask for opinions	Interrupt politely	Focus the discussion
• What do you think about … ? • Would you like to add something, (*name*)? • How would you respond, (*name*)?	• Thank you, (*name of person speaking*). Would you like to add anything, (*name of a quiet person*)? • Would anyone else like to say something?	• Let's get back on topic. • Remember, we are discussing (*state topic / question*). • I'd like to keep the discussion on track.

A. Go online to listen to a group discussion about business advice. Complete the conversation with the phrases you hear. Compare your answers with a partner. Practice reading the conversation in a small group.

Jamie: _____ *Let's get back on topic.* _____ Our group is supposed to talk
(1)

about question four: Which piece of business advice do you think is best and

why? _____
(2)

Theresa: I agree with the first point about making a business plan. It seems

like an important first step.

Robin: Maybe. But I think the best piece of advice is to do what you love. My

uncle had a food market, and he was really interested in new products, so it

was the perfect job for…

Jamie: _____
(3)

Vicki: Yes. I agree with Theresa about the business plan. I also wanted to say

that the last piece of advice may not always work. Sometimes when you listen

to your intuition, it can be wrong.

Jamie: That's a good point. _____
(4)

Brenda: I think the best advice was that you shouldn't try to start a new

business alone. We always need help from our family and friends.

B. In a small group, discuss the following questions. Choose a different facilitator for each discussion. Practice asking for opinions, interrupting politely, and focusing the discussion.

1. Who is your role model and why?
2. What is the best way to prepare for a long vacation?
3. If you had a long weekend with no homework, how would you spend your time?

LEARN

English | speakers | do | not | speak | word | by | word: *They—run—their—words—together.* Following a few guidelines for linking—or connecting—words will help you to speak naturally and smoothly.

A. Read the expressions for maintaining a conversation and keeping a discussion focused. Notice how words ending in a consonant sound are linked to words beginning with a vowel. Go online to listen to the examples. Repeat them.

What do you think—about ... ?

How do you feel—about ... ?

Can you say more—about that?

Would—anyone like to

comment—on that?

Let's hear from someone—else.

PRONUNCIATION TIPS

Keep your voice going. Don't stop between words.

Hold on!   →   Hol—don!

Wait a minute!   →   Wai—da minute!

Let's get back on track.   →   Let's get ba—ckon track.

B. Look at the chart. Notice how some consonants combine to form a new sound. Go online to listen and repeat.

t + y = ch	/ts/ + y = ch	d + y = j
whatchu	whatcher	wouldju
I don't see what—you mean.	What's—your point?	How would—you respond?

C. Connect vowel sounds with /w/ or /y/. Go online to listen. Repeat what you hear.

Do you—agree with that?   Can you give me—an example?

APPLY

A. Go online to listen. Check (✓) the sound you hear.

	w	y
1. May—I ask you something?		✓
2. Can you give us a few—ideas?		
3. Why—is that, do you think?		
4. Let's stay—on topic.		
5. Can you—explain that?		
6. Oh,—I get it!		

B. Use guidelines in Learn, activities A, B, and C to link words. Check your answers with a partner.

Would you agree?

I'm not sure I follow.

What's your feeling?

We're going off topic.

Would you like to add anything?

Could you tell me more about that?

Would anyone else like to say something?

Could you expand on that?

May I interrupt you for a moment?

C. Practice linking the expressions in Apply, activity A. Listen and repeat. Then practice with a partner.

Wouldjuwa → *Wouldjuwagree?*

End of Unit Task

In this unit, you learned to recognize persuasive speech and facilitate a discussion. Listen to a persuasive speech and participate in a group discussion.

A. Review helpful phrases for facilitating a discussion and answer the questions below.

Ask for opinions	Interrupt politely	Focus the discussion
· What do you think about … ? · Would you like to add something, *(name)*? · How would you respond, *(name)*? · Would you agree that … ?	· Thank you, *(name of person speaking)*. Would you like to add anything, *(name of a quiet person)*? · OK, let's hear from someone else. · Would anyone else like to say something?	· Let's get back on topic. · Remember, we are discussing *(state topic / question)*. · I'd like to keep the discussion on track.

1. During a group discussion of an article about customer service, one student begins by talking about an experience she had at a clothing store. She then starts talking about her favorite clothes. What phrases could you use to focus the discussion?

2. In the same discussion, what are some phrases you could use to politely interrupt the student who is speaking off topic?

3. During a group discussion of successful businesses, your classmate Ramon is very quiet. What are some phrases you could use to get him to participate?

B. Go online to listen to a speech about putting a restaurant on campus. In the chart, write down examples of persuasive speech you hear.

Clues about the speaker's opinion	Positive or negative words	Personalized language	Rhetorical questions

C. Analyze your notes. What does the speaker want you to believe or do? Discuss your ideas with a partner.

D. If you were a student at that school, would this speech persuade you to support building a restaurant on campus? Why or why not? Which of the speaker's arguments were most effective? Not effective? Discuss with a partner.

E. Complete the following sentence: I (do / do not) support building a restaurant on campus because _____. Discuss with a partner.

F. Participate in a group discussion about the speech. Work in a group of 3–5 students. Choose one student to be the facilitator. The facilitator's job is to include all speakers, ask for opinions, and keep the discussion focused on the topic.

Self-Assessment		
Yes	No	
☐	☐	I successfully recognized words with positive or negative meanings.
☐	☐	I successfully identified persuasive speech.
☐	☐	I actively participated in a group discussion.
☐	☐	I successfully facilitated a group discussion.
☐	☐	I can link words when speaking.
☐	☐	I can correctly use the target vocabulary words from the unit.

Discussion Questions

With a partner or in a small group, discuss the following questions.

1. What do you need to do to start a franchise?
2. What are the advantages of having a franchise instead of starting your own business?
3. Why would someone not want to have a franchise?

10

Hidden Treasure

In this unit, you will

> learn about the sport of geocaching.
> increase your understanding of the target academic words for this unit.

LISTENING AND SPEAKING SKILLS

> Synthesizing Information
> Participating in a Debate
> **PRONUNCIATION** Constrastive Stress

Self-Assessment

Think about how well you know each target word, and check (✓) the appropriate column. I have…

TARGET WORDS	never seen this word before.	heard or seen the word but am not sure what it means.	heard or seen the word and understand what it means.	used the word confidently in *either* speaking or writing.
AWL				
compound				
🔑 concept				
displace				
equate				
🔑 impose				
🔑 interpret				
🔑 interval				
manual				
passive				
🔑 principle				
ratio				
🔑 stable				
🔑 unique				
voluntary				

🔑 Oxford 3000™ keywords

Vocabulary Activities

A. Complete each sentence with the correct verb form and tense of *interpret*, *misinterpret*, or *reinterpret*.

1. Mr. Wang was upset that the employees had *misinterpreted* his instructions.

2. The trail map was difficult to _____ because the trail lengths weren't drawn accurately.

3. In order for a person to find geocaches, a GPS device has to _____ the cache's coordinates.

4. The Peters Projection Word Map offers a(n) _____ of the traditional world map. In it, country sizes are shown in their true proportions.

5. The vehicle's GPS device _____ the address and directed the driver to the wrong location.

B. Complete the Word Form Chart below with the correct forms of the target words. Use a dictionary to check your answers.

concept	displace	interval	stabilize
conceptual	displaced	stability	stable
conceptually	displacement	stabilization	

Word Form Chart			
Noun	**Verb**	**Adjective**	**Adverb**
concept			

Word Form Chart			
Noun	**Verb**	**Adjective**	**Adverb**
equation	equate	_____	_____
principle	_____	principled unprincipled	_____
volunteer	volunteer	voluntary	voluntarily

C. Using the target words in the Word Form Chart on page 110, complete this paragraph. Be sure to use the correct form and tense of each word.

In geocaching, in order for people to find hidden items, _volunteers_ need
                                                              (1)
to hide them. Often, geocachers themselves _____ hide the items
                                                  (2)
for other players. The _____ is that for every item a person finds,
                          (3)
he / she should hide a new item. It's a balanced _____. People take
                                                       (4)
one and leave one. Geocaching continues as a sport because its players are

_____ people. They know that if they don't contribute, there won't
      (5)
be items to find. That's why players _____ so much of their free time.
                                           (6)
They want the sport to continue.

D. Cross out the form of *concept* that is incorrect in each sentence.

1. Mapping population growth, instead of just landmass, is a recent
   concept / conceptually in geography.

2. Some early *conceptualization / conceptual* maps of the world showed only
   the northern hemisphere.

3. *Conceptualize / Conceptually*, medieval maps of the known world are
   interesting, but they aren't very accurate.

Manual is an adjective that means "using your hands" or "operated by
hand." The adverb form is *manually*.

> My new car has a **manual** transmission.

> Sasha had to use the keyboard to enter the information **manually**.

As a noun, *manual* means "a book that explains how to do or operate
something."

> I'm glad the camera came with a **manual**. Otherwise, I wouldn't know how to use it.

CORPUS

E. Read the following sentences. With a partner, decide if you would restate each
sentence with the adverb or noun form of *manual*.

_____adverb_____ 1. The washing machine broke, so we had to wash the clothes in
                    the sink.

_____ 2. I read the pamphlet that came with my computer, but I still don't
                    know how to fix it.

_____ 3. Before computers, mapmakers worked with pen and paper.

About the Topic

Geocaching is a sport in which people, called geocachers, look for items other geocachers hide in public places. The items, such as wooden tokens or plastic toys, are not valuable. The excitement comes from searching for them. People use hand-held GPS (Global Positioning System) devices or apps on their smartphones to the find the locations of the items.

Before You Watch

Read these questions. Discuss your answers in a small group.

1. Do you like to search for hidden items?
2. Why do you think people like to search for hidden items?
3. Have you ever used a GPS device? If so, what for?

 ## Watch

Read the Listen for Main Ideas activity below. Go online to watch news clips about the sport of geocaching.

 ## Listen for Main Ideas

Read the questions about the video. Work with a partner to ask and answer these questions.

1. How do people use GPS in geocaching?
2. Why are the people in the video excited about geocaching?
3. What kind of data do people need to interpret for geocaching?
4. What happens after geocachers find a hidden cache?
5. What is the most important principle geocachers follow?

LEARN

Synthesizing information means combining many parts to make a logical whole. Students often receive information about one topic from multiple sources. For example, your professor may ask you to read an article about a specific place and then show you a video about it. Each source probably has some information that the other one does not. As you review your notes, you will want to make connections between the two sources. This is called *synthesizing information*. After synthesizing, you may be able to make conclusions that you could not make with just one source of information.

A. Read the example of *synthesized* information. Information from both sources, the magazine and video, are necessary to come to the conclusion.

Information from *Outdoor Excursions* magazine:	Information from *Adventure Quest* video:
• Tourists love that Buenos Aires, Argentina, has an average annual temperature of 64 degrees Fahrenheit. • Los Angeles, California, has warm summers and mild winters that make it a perfect travel destination.	• Buenos Aires and Los Angeles are approximately 6,000 miles apart. • Both cities are a nearly equal distance from the equator.

Even though they are far apart, Buenos Aires and Los Angeles both have nice weather because they are similar distances from the equator.

APPLY

A. Ask five of your classmates these questions and record their answers. Next, compare and contrast your classmates' responses. Finally, *synthesize* the information to make generally true statements about your classmates.

1. What time did you leave home this morning?

2. What will you do after this class?

3. How much time do you spend doing homework each day?

B. The people in the video are sources of information about geocaching. Watch the video again and take notes on the information each person gives. *Synthesize* the information you heard in order to write at least two conclusions based on both sources.

_____

_____

_____

C. Work with a partner. Compare your conclusions.

Vocabulary Activities

Word Form Chart

Noun	Verb	Adjective	Adverb
compound	compound	compounding	_____
imposition	impose	imposing	_____
manual	_____	manual	manually
passivity	_____	passive	passively
ratio	_____	_____	_____
uniqueness	_____	unique	uniquely

A. Using the target words in the Word Form Chart, complete the paragraph below. Be sure to use the correct form and tense of each word.

National parks are a treasure for any country. These parks capture the beauty and individuality of the local natural world. They also preserve that beauty and ___*uniqueness*___ for future generations. To minimize the negative impact

(1)

people have on these places, park rangers have to _____ certain

(2)

rules. Visitors can use tents or stay in recreational _____ created by

(3)

the rangers. These _____ have wooden cabins that visitors can stay

(4)

in overnight. Overnight camping in some national parks is a _____

(5)

experience because park rangers put on shows to entertain overnight

campers. The _____ of visitors to rangers is 20-to-1, so rangers often

(6)

entertain large groups of people. The rangers discourage _____ by

(7)

making these shows active for the visitors. Visitors often go on night hikes

and identify nocturnal, or nighttime, animals. In the morning, visitors can

_____ enter the names of the animals they identified into a database.

(8)

Visitors enjoy the work; it's not an _____ on them. It's part of the

(9)

effort to identify, count, and protect the animals that live in the park.

Everyone has a role to play in preserving these national parks.

The word *compound* has slightly different meanings depending on its context.

A *compound* refers to "an area surrounded by a fence or wall in which a group of buildings stands."

(1) Geocachers hide caches in old military **compounds**.

Additionally, *compound* may refer to "a substance formed by a chemical reaction of two or more elements in fixed amounts relative to each other."

(2) Water is a **compound** made of two hydrogen atoms and one oxygen atom.

The word can also mean "a noun, adjective, or verb made of two or more words."

(3) Homework is an example of a **compound** noun.

CORPUS

B. Using the sample definitions above, list different words related to each meaning (1–3) of *compound* discussed above. Explain your answers to a partner.

Compound (1)	Compound (2)	Compound (3)
1. military compound	1. water	1. homework
2.	2.	2.
3.	3.	3.

C. Complete the following sentences using the correct form of *impose*. When finished, discuss with a partner what it means to be in an imposing *situation*.

1. Monitoring geocaches can sometimes be an ___imposition___ for park rangers.

2. When geocachers don't ask before hiding their caches in national parks, they _____ on the park rangers' goodwill.

3. It can be an _____ to ask park rangers to bend park rules to accommodate geocaching.

4. Borrowing someone's GPS device to geocache is an _____ if you don't return it promptly!

D. Find the most appropriate synonym and antonym for each target word from the list of words below.

	synonym	antonym	
1. compound	combined	separate	(closed / combined / individual / separate)
2. passive	_____	_____	(shy / assertive / uninvolved / thoughtful)
3. unique	_____	_____	(distinct / accurate / faithful / common)

About the Topic

A national park is land set aside for people to enjoy. Park rangers work in national parks to ensure the parks' rules are followed. An important rule is people cannot leave litter, or trash, in a park. Another rule is that these public spaces should be left as they were found. These spaces have always been natural and wild, and they should be left that way for future generations to view and enjoy.

Before You Listen

Read these questions. Discuss your answers in a small group.

1. Do you know or can you think of any rules people have to follow when visiting national parks?

2. When do you make exceptions to rules?

3. Are there places people shouldn't be allowed to hide geocaches? Explain.

Listen

Read the Listen for Main Ideas activity below. Go online to listen to a student debate about geocaching in national parks.

Listening for Main Ideas

Read the questions about the debate. Work with a partner to ask and answer these questions.

1. What is one possible negative effect of geocaching in national parks?

2. According to the students, how are geocaches different from litter?

3. What are the debaters' opinions about making an exception to park rules regarding geocaches?

4. What are two arguments for each side of the debate?

PRESENTATION SKILL | Participating in a Debate

LEARN

A classroom debate is a well-organized argument about an issue. Students are assigned to one of two teams, either affirmative or negative. The affirmative team, sometimes called *for*, argues in favor of something and the negative team, sometimes called *against*, argues against it.

Debates can have a variety of formats. One simple format begins with each team making an opening statement of its argument. This is when the team explains whether it is *for* or *against* the topic of debate. Good arguments should be supported by facts. Next, each team gives a rebuttal. This is when they respond directly to their opponent's arguments. Finally, each team summarizes its arguments in a closing statement. The audience (or instructor) usually votes to decide which team wins.

Debates give you an opportunity to use many academic skills, such as supporting your opinion with facts (unit 2), summarizing information (unit 3), being concise (unit 5), and citing information (unit 8).

In a debate, you should respond directly to your opponent's arguments. Use the following phrases in your rebuttal.

Useful debate phrases
My opponent argues that ... , but ...
You heard ... . In fact, ...
I disagree that ... because ...
It is not the case that ... . In reality, ...
It may be true that ... , but ...

A. Go online to listen again to the audio. Add any useful debate phrases to this list.

APPLY

A. Choose one of the topics below to discuss with a partner. Decide who is for (answers "yes" to the question) and who is against (answers "no" to the question) the issue.

1. Should students be allowed to use cell phones in school?
2. Should military service be mandatory?
3. Is vegetarianism healthier than eating meat?

B. Write an opening statement that includes:

1. The topic of your debate

   Today we are debating whether students should be allowed to use cell phones in school.

2. A short summary of both positions.

   Some people argue that ...

3. Your position on the issue and two or three facts that support your position.

   I am (for / against) cell phone use in schools because ...

C. Present your opening statements to the class. Ask your classmates to give you feedback.

LEARN

Writers use punctuation and formatting to draw special attention to contrasting words. Speakers use stress to emphasize differences. Effective English speakers signal contrast by making some words stronger, longer, and often higher than usual. This is called contrastive stress.

Reading / Writing	Listening / Speaking
"Does she *like* it?" asked Shane.	Shane: Does she like it?
"She *loves* it!" cried Monica.	Monica: She loves it!

A. Go online to listen to a dialogue between a customer and server at a restaurant. Notice the relation between stress, focus, and the speakers' intentions.

Normal focus	Special focus	
Stress the last content word	**Stress contrasting words**	**Speaker's intention**
A: Hi! How are you?	B: Fine, how are you?	Returning questions
A: Good. Can I get a large coke?	B: Sure. Do you want that with or without ice?	Showing contrast
A: Whatever's quickest.	B: OK. That'll be $1.70 with tax. Sorry! $1.75.	Correcting information

B. Go online to listen to everyday conversations. Notice how Speaker B returns Speaker A's question by shifting the stress.

1. A: How's it going?
   B: Great! How's it going with you?
2. A: Hey! What's up?
   B: Not too much. What's up with you?
3. A: What did you do over the weekend?
   B: I hung out at home. What about you?
4. A: How was your vacation?
   B: Wonderful! How was yours?

APPLY

A. Go online to listen to the dialogues and fill in the missing words in the chart on page 119. Then practice with a partner.

Showing contrast	Correcting information
A: What's your position on texting in class? Are you **for** it or (1) _against_ it?	A: So I'll see you at (1) _____ ?
	B: (2) _____ ? I thought we said (3) _____ .
B. Definitely (2) _____ it. Students should be studying, not (3) _____ . Besides, **some** people would argue that it's rude and disrespectful to the teacher.	A: We did? Well, OK. (4) _____ , then. At the (5) _____ .
	B: I'm pretty sure we said we'd meet at a (6) _____ .

B. You are Speaker B. Listen to Speaker A and respond. "Return" their statement by shifting the stress. (Do not add extra words!) Compare your stress with the audio model. Then practice with a partner.

1. Nice to meet you.   *Speaker B: Nice to **meet** you.*

2. Nice to see you.   *Speaker B: Nice to meet **you.***

3. Nice talking to you.   *Speaker B: Nice talking to **you.***

4. Thank you.   *Speaker B: Thank **you**!*

C. Practice the dialogues in Learn, activities A and B with a partner. Make contrasting words extra long and extra high.

End of Unit Task

In this unit, you learned how to debate items and synthesize information you hear. Practice both of these skills by participating and listening to a debate.

A. Half of the class will participate in a debate while the other half listens and takes notes. The debate question is: Should the driving age be raised to 21? The *for* team believes it should be raised. The *against* team argues there should be no change.

DEBATERS

B. If you are a debater, prepare with a partner. Brainstorm three arguments *for* and *against* raising the driving age to 21. You will be on one side of the debate, but it is good to think about your opponent's arguments, too.

For	Against

C. Debate your points while your classmates listen and take notes.

D. When you finish the debate, look at the questions under the heading "Everyone" on page 120.

LISTENERS

A. While the debaters are preparing, predict what arguments you think you will hear from each side of the debate.

B. If you are debating, review the debate phrases on page 117. Use them in your argument. Decide with a partner who will take notes about the *for* team and who will take notes on the *against* team. (Together you and your partner will have complete notes for both sides of the debate.)

C. Listen carefully and take notes on the team you've selected. Your partner will take notes on the other team's arguments.

D. After the debate, synthesize the information in your notes with a partner.

EVERYONE

A. Discuss the following questions.

1. What was the best argument made by the *for* team?
2. What facts or expert opinions did they use to support their arguments?
3. What was the best argument made by the *against* team?
4. What facts or expert opinions did they use to support their arguments?
5. Did each team respond to the other team's arguments?

B. If you have time, switch roles. Debaters become listeners. Listeners become debaters. Discuss the question: Should the government limit the size of salable sugary drinks like soda?

Self-Assessment		
Yes	**No**	
☐	☐	I successfully participated in a debate and used at least two useful debate phrases.
☐	☐	I took careful notes about one team's arguments during the debate.
☐	☐	I synthesized information about the debate from my notes and my partner's notes.
☐	☐	I used information in my notes to explain my decision about who won the debate.
☐	☐	I can use contrastive stress.
☐	☐	I can correctly use the target vocabulary words from the unit.

Discussion Questions

With a partner or in a small group, discuss the following questions.

1. What would a person need to do to start a geocaching hunt in his / her city or town?
2. What skills does a person need to have in order to go geocaching?
3. How would geocaching compare to treasure hunting?

The Academic Word List

Words targeted in Level 3 are bold

Word	Sublist	Location
abandon	8	L2, U4
abstract	**6**	**L3, U3**
academy	5	L2, U10
access	4	L0, U5
accommodate	**9**	**L3, U6**
accompany	8	L4, U2
accumulate	**8**	**L3, U4**
accurate	6	L0, U2
achieve	2	L0, U4
acknowledge	6	L0, U7
acquire	**2**	**L3, U9**
adapt	**7**	**L3, U7**
adequate	**4**	**L3, U9**
adjacent	10	L4, U4
adjust	5	L4, U4
administrate	2	L4, U8
adult	7	L0, U10
advocate	7	L4, U3
affect	2	L1, U1
aggregate	6	L4, U6
aid	7	L0, U5
albeit	10	L4, U3
allocate	**6**	**L3, U6**
alter	5	L2, U6
alternative	3	L1, U1
ambiguous	8	L4, U7
amend	5	L4, U7
analogy	9	L4, U1
analyze	1	L1, U3
annual	4	L1, U9
anticipate	9	L2, U8
apparent	4	L2, U4
append	8	L4, U10
appreciate	8	L0, U9
approach	1	L1, U1
appropriate	**2**	**L3, U5**
approximate	4	L2, U7
arbitrary	8	L4, U7
area	**1**	**L3, U7**
aspect	2	L2, U7
assemble	**10**	**L3, U1**
assess	1	L2, U8
assign	**6**	**L3, U5**
assist	2	L0, U2
assume	**1**	**L3, U1**
assure	9	L4, U8
attach	6	L0, U10

Word	Sublist	Location
attain	**9**	**L3, U5**
attitude	4	L2, U4
attribute	**4**	**L3, U8**
author	6	L0, U1
authority	1	L2, U2
automate	8	L2, U1
available	1	L0, U8
aware	5	L1, U1
behalf	9	L4, U9
benefit	1	L1, U2
bias	8	L4, U3
bond	6	L4, U9
brief	6	L2, U9
bulk	**9**	**L3, U1**
capable	**6**	**L3, U5**
capacity	**5**	**L3, U2**
category	2	L2, U4
cease	9	L2, U2
challenge	5	L1, U6
channel	7	L4, U5
chapter	2	L0, U2
chart	8	L0, U2
chemical	7	L2, U6
circumstance	3	L4, U2
cite	6	L4, U4
civil	**4**	**L3, U2**
clarify	**8**	**L3, U7**
classic	**7**	**L3, U6**
clause	5	L4, U8
code	4	L0, U5
coherent	9	L4, U7
coincide	9	L4, U10
collapse	**10**	**L3, U9**
colleague	10	L1, U5
commence	9	L2, U4
comment	3	L1, U4
commission	**2**	**L3, U2**
commit	4	L2, U1
commodity	8	L4, U4
communicate	4	L1, U3
community	2	L1, U4
compatible	9	L2, U4
compensate	3	L4, U8
compile	10	L4, U9
complement	8	L4, U8

Word	Sublist	Location
🔑 complex	2	L2, U1
🔑 **component**	**3**	**L3, U1**
compound	**5**	**L3, U10**
comprehensive	7	L2, U6
comprise	**7**	**L3, U7**
compute	2	L1, U8
conceive	10	L4, U7
🔑 concentrate	4	L1, U5
🔑 **concept**	**1**	**L3, U10**
🔑 conclude	2	L0, U6
concurrent	9	L4, U10
🔑 conduct	2	L1, U4
confer	4	L4, U8
confine	9	L4, U8
🔑 confirm	7	L1, U8
🔑 conflict	5	L1, U7
conform	**8**	**L3, U6**
consent	**3**	**L3, U3**
consequent	2	L4, U2
🔑 considerable	3	L4, U1
🔑 consist	1	L1, U9
🔑 constant	3	L1, U8
constitute	1	L4, U5
constrain	3	L4, U6
🔑 **construct**	**2**	**L3, U1**
🔑 consult	5	L2, U8
consume	2	L2, U6
🔑 contact	5	L1, U4
🔑 contemporary	8	L4, U6
🔑 context	1	L2, U4
🔑 **contract**	**1**	**L3, U4**
contradict	8	L2, U4
contrary	**7**	**L3, U1**
🔑 **contrast**	**4**	**L3, U2**
🔑 contribute	3	L1, U9
controversy	9	L2, U9
convene	3	L4, U1
converse	9	L2, U2
🔑 **convert**	**7**	**L3, U3**
🔑 convince	10	L1, U5
cooperate	**6**	**L3, U6**
coordinate	3	L2, U2
🔑 core	3	L4, U10
corporate	3	L1, U7
correspond	3	L2, U10
🔑 couple	7	L0, U4
🔑 **create**	**1**	**L3, U7**
🔑 credit	2	L2, U7
🔑 **criteria**	**3**	**L3, U2**
🔑 **crucial**	**8**	**L3, U7**
🔑 culture	2	L0, U10

Word	Sublist	Location
currency	8	L2, U3
🔑 **cycle**	**4**	**L3, U5**
🔑 data	1	L0, U4
🔑 **debate**	**4**	**L3, U5**
🔑 decade	7	L1, U9
🔑 decline	5	L1, U9
deduce	3	L4, U10
🔑 define	1	L0, U8
🔑 definite	7	L4, U8
🔑 demonstrate	3	L1, U2
denote	8	L4, U10
🔑 deny	7	L1, U8
🔑 depress	10	L0, U8
🔑 derive	1	L4, U8
🔑 design	2	L0, U10
🔑 **despite**	**4**	**L3, U6**
detect	8	L2, U3
deviate	8	L4, U10
🔑 device	9	L0, U2
🔑 devote	9	L2, U3
differentiate	**7**	**L3, U6**
dimension	4	L4, U9
diminish	9	L2, U8
discrete	5	L4, U2
discriminate	6	L4, U5
displace	**8**	**L3, U10**
🔑 display	6	L0, U8
dispose	7	L4, U1
distinct	2	L4, U2
distort	9	L4, U5
🔑 distribute	1	L1, U9
diverse	**6**	**L3, U2**
🔑 document	3	L0, U4
domain	6	L4, U6
🔑 domestic	4	L2, U5
🔑 **dominate**	**3**	**L3, U7**
🔑 draft	5	L0, U10
🔑 drama	8	L2, U9
duration	9	L2, U3
dynamic	**7**	**L3, U3**
🔑 economy	1	L2, U8
edit	6	L1, U7
🔑 **element**	**2**	**L3, U1**
🔑 eliminate	7	L1, U6
🔑 **emerge**	**4**	**L3, U5**
🔑 emphasis	3	L1, U5
empirical	7	L4, U4
🔑 enable	5	L2, U1
🔑 encounter	10	L1, U8

🔑 Oxford 3000™ words

Word	Sublist	Location
energy	5	L0, U9
enforce	5	L4, U1
enhance	**6**	**L3, U2**
enormous	10	L0, U7
ensure	3	L4, U1
entity	5	L4, U8
environment	1	L1, U1
equate	**2**	**L3, U10**
equip	7	L2, U1
equivalent	5	L1, U7
erode	9	L4, U2
error	4	L0, U2
establish	1	L2, U5
estate	6	L4, U8
estimate	1	L2, U5
ethic	**9**	**L3, U4**
ethnic	4	L3, U9
evaluate	2	L1, U8
eventual	**8**	**L3, U2**
evident	1	L2, U8
evolve	5	L2, U2
exceed	6	L1, U10
exclude	**3**	**L3, U8**
exhibit	8	L2, U3
expand	5	L0, U5
expert	6	L0, U3
explicit	6	L4, U3
exploit	8	L4, U9
export	1	L4, U6
expose	5	L4, U1
external	5	L2, U1
extract	**7**	**L3, U1**
facilitate	**5**	**L3, U6**
factor	1	L3, U1
feature	2	L0, U2
federal	6	L4, U4
fee	6	L0, U5
file	7	L0, U5
final	2	L0, U1
finance	**1**	**L3, U6**
finite	7	L4, U9
flexible	6	L1, U10
fluctuate	8	L4, U10
focus	2	L0, U6
format	9	L2, U8
formula	**1**	**L3, U5**
forthcoming	10	L4, U10
found	9	L0, U7
foundation	7	L1, U9
framework	3	L4, U6

Word	Sublist	Location
function	**1**	**L3, U3**
fund	3	L2, U5
fundamental	5	L1, U8
furthermore	**6**	**L3, U4**
gender	**6**	**L3, U8**
generate	5	L1, U5
generation	5	L2, U10
globe	7	L2, U5
goal	4	L0, U7
grade	7	L0, U3
grant	**4**	**L3, U9**
guarantee	7	L1, U7
guideline	8	L1, U6
hence	**4**	**L3, U6**
hierarchy	7	L4, U6
highlight	8	L0, U7
hypothesis	**4**	**L3, U4**
identical	**7**	**L3, U3**
identify	1	L1, U3
ideology	7	L4, U3
ignorance	6	L2, U9
illustrate	3	L0, U1
image	5	L1, U3
immigrate	3	L4, U7
impact	2	L2, U9
implement	4	L4, U2
implicate	4	L4, U3
implicit	8	L4, U3
imply	**3**	**L3, U8**
impose	**4**	**L3, U10**
incentive	6	L4, U2
incidence	**6**	**L3, U4**
incline	10	L4, U4
income	1	L0, U4
incorporate	6	L4, U9
index	6	L4, U9
indicate	1	L2, U10
individual	1	L0, U1
induce	8	L4, U1
inevitable	**8**	**L3, U2**
infer	7	L4, U3
infrastructure	8	L4, U1
inherent	9	L4, U7
inhibit	6	L4, U2
initial	3	L0, U3
initiate	**6**	**L3, U8**
injure	2	L4, U9
innovate	**7**	**L3, U1**

Oxford 3000™ words

Word	Sublist	Location	Word	Sublist	Location
input	6	L2, U5	maximize	3	L1, U9
insert	7	L2, U7	**mechanism**	**4**	**L3, U3**
insight	**9**	**L3, U4**	media	7	L0, U8
inspect	8	L4, U9	mediate	9	L4, U10
instance	**3**	**L3, U3**	medical	5	L1, U2
institute	2	L1, U6	medium	9	L1, U10
instruct	6	L1, U6	mental	5	L2, U6
integral	9	L4, U6	method	1	L1, U2
integrate	4	L4, U6	migrate	6	L4, U1
integrity	10	L2, U1	military	9	L2, U3
intelligence	6	L0, U10	minimal	9	L1, U9
intense	**8**	**L3, U7**	**minimize**	**8**	**L3, U1**
interact	3	L2, U3	minimum	6	L1, U10
intermediate	9	L2, U5	ministry	6	L4, U6
internal	4	L1, U10	minor	3	L0, U7
interpret	**1**	**L3, U10**	mode	7	L4, U5
interval	**6**	**L3, U10**	modify	5	L1, U6
intervene	**7**	**L3, U6**	**monitor**	**5**	**L3, U4**
intrinsic	10	L4, U7	motive	6	L2, U7
invest	**2**	**L3, U2**	mutual	9	L2, U2
investigate	4	L2, U9			
invoke	10	L4, U5	negate	3	L4, U4
involve	**1**	**L3, U7**	network	5	L2, U2
isolate	**7**	**L3, U2**	neutral	6	L2, U5
issue	1	L0, U3	**nevertheless**	**6**	**L3, U5**
item	2	L0, U6	nonetheless	10	L4, U5
			norm	9	L4, U7
job	4	L0, U10	normal	2	L0, U6
journal	2	L1, U10	**notion**	**5**	**L3, U5**
justify	3	L4, U2	notwithstanding	10	L4, U6
			nuclear	**8**	**L3, U9**
label	4	L0, U1			
labor	1	L2, U4	objective	5	L0, U4
layer	**3**	**L3, U3**	**obtain**	**2**	**L3, U4**
lecture	6	L0, U6	obvious	4	L1, U7
legal	1	L1, U2	occupy	4	L4, U8
legislate	1	L4, U1	occur	1	L2, U10
levy	10	L4, U3	odd	10	L1, U8
liberal	5	L4, U3	offset	8	L4, U9
license	**5**	**L3, U8**	ongoing	10	L2, U7
likewise	**10**	**L3, U4**	option	4	L1, U10
link	3	L0, U4	orient	5	L4, U4
locate	3	L1, U4	outcome	3	L2, U7
logic	**5**	**L3, U5**	output	4	L2, U5
			overall	4	L2, U9
maintain	2	L1, U10	overlap	9	L2, U4
major	**1**	**L3, U7**	overseas	6	L2, U3
manipulate	8	L4, U10			
manual	**9**	**L3, U10**	panel	10	L4, U5
margin	5	L2, U3	paradigm	7	L4, U2
mature	9	L2, U8	paragraph	8	L1, U7

Word	Sublist	Location
🔑 parallel	4	L4, U3
parameter	**4**	**L3, U4**
🔑 participate	2	L1, U2
🔑 partner	3	L0, U3
passive	**9**	**L3, U10**
perceive	**2**	**L3, U7**
🔑 percent	1	L1, U3
🔑 **period**	**1**	**L3, U3**
persist	**10**	**L3, U4**
🔑 perspective	5	L2, U10
🔑 phase	4	L2, U10
phenomenon	7	L4, U4
🔑 **philosophy**	**3**	**L3, U8**
🔑 physical	3	L0, U1
🔑 plus	8	L0, U6
🔑 policy	1	L2, U9
portion	9	L2, U6
🔑 pose	10	L4, U4
🔑 positive	2	L0, U7
🔑 potential	2	L2, U10
practitioner	8	L4, U1
precede	**6**	**L3, U9**
🔑 **precise**	**5**	**L3, U3**
🔑 predict	4	L0, U9
predominant	8	L4, U5
preliminary	9	L2, U2
presume	6	L4, U7
🔑 previous	2	L0, U9
🔑 primary	2	L1, U3
prime	5	L4, U2
🔑 principal	4	L2, U10
🔑 **principle**	**1**	**L3, U10**
🔑 prior	4	L2, U8
🔑 priority	7	L2, U6
🔑 proceed	1	L2, U1
🔑 process	1	L1, U2
🔑 professional	4	L1, U2
prohibit	**7**	**L3, U2**
🔑 project	4	L1, U9
🔑 promote	4	L4, U7
🔑 proportion	3	L2, U8
🔑 prospect	8	L4, U6
protocol	9	L4, U9
psychology	5	L2, U8
🔑 **publication**	**7**	**L3, U9**
🔑 publish	3	L0, U1
🔑 purchase	2	L0, U7
🔑 pursue	5	L4, U4
qualitative	9	L4, U8
🔑 quote	7	L1, U7

Word	Sublist	Location
radical	8	L4, U5
random	8	L2, U5
🔑 range	2	L2, U10
ratio	**5**	**L3, U10**
rational	**6**	**L3, U9**
🔑 react	3	L1, U3
🔑 recover	6	L2, U1
refine	**9**	**L3, U5**
regime	**4**	**L3, U9**
🔑 region	2	L2, U2
🔑 **register**	**3**	**L3, U8**
regulate	2	L2, U2
reinforce	**8**	**L3, U4**
🔑 reject	5	L1, U10
🔑 relax	9	L0, U6
🔑 release	7	L2, U5
🔑 **relevant**	**2**	**L3, U8**
reluctant	10	L2, U3
🔑 rely	3	L2, U9
🔑 remove	3	L0, U9
🔑 require	1	L0, U10
🔑 research	1	L0, U3
reside	2	L4, U3
🔑 resolve	4	L2, U4
🔑 resource	2	L0, U3
🔑 respond	1	L1, U4
🔑 restore	8	L2, U10
restrain	**9**	**L3, U9**
🔑 restrict	2	L2, U7
🔑 retain	4	L4, U7
🔑 reveal	6	L2, U1
revenue	**5**	**L3, U6**
🔑 **reverse**	**7**	**L3, U9**
🔑 revise	8	L1, U7
🔑 **revolution**	**9**	**L3, U3**
rigid	9	L2, U6
🔑 role	1	L0, U9
🔑 **route**	**9**	**L3, U9**
scenario	9	L2, U7
🔑 schedule	7	L1, U5
scheme	**3**	**L3, U2**
scope	6	L2, U9
🔑 section	1	L0, U9
🔑 sector	1	L4, U6
🔑 secure	2	L1, U6
🔑 seek	2	L2, U7
🔑 select	2	L1, U4
sequence	3	L1, U6
🔑 series	4	L0, U9
🔑 sex	3	L4, U4

🔑 Oxford 3000™ words

Word	Sublist	Location
shift	3	L2, U7
significant	**1**	**L3, U2**
similar	1	L1, U5
simulate	**7**	**L3, U4**
site	2	L0, U5
so-called	10	L2, U9
sole	7	L4, U10
somewhat	**7**	**L3, U7**
source	1	L1, U1
specific	1	L1, U6
specify	3	L1, U8
sphere	9	L4, U6
stable	**5**	**L3, U10**
statistic	**4**	**L3, U8**
status	4	L0, U4
straightforward	**10**	**L3, U6**
strategy	2	L2, U2
stress	**4**	**L3, U7**
structure	1	L2, U1
style	5	L2, U2
submit	7	L1, U10
subordinate	9	L4, U3
subsequent	**4**	**L3, U5**
subsidy	6	L4, U8
substitute	5	L2, U3
successor	**7**	**L3, U6**
sufficient	3	L4, U2
sum	**4**	**L3, U9**
summary	4	L1, U3
supplement	9	L2, U6
survey	2	L2, U6
survive	7	L2, U9
suspend	9	L4, U5
sustain	**5**	**L3, U1**
symbol	5	L0, U8
tape	**6**	**L3, U8**
target	5	L2, U6
task	3	L0, U5
team	9	L0, U3
technical	**3**	**L3, U3**
technique	**3**	**L3, U5**
technology	3	L2, U10
temporary	9	L0, U8
tense	7	L2, U6
terminate	7	L4, U10
text	2	L0, U1
theme	7	L1, U5
theory	**1**	**L3, U8**
thereby	7	L4, U7
thesis	7	L4, U7

Word	Sublist	Location
topic	7	L0, U6
trace	6	L4, U5
tradition	2	L0, U2
transfer	2	L1, U6
transform	**6**	**L3, U1**
transit	5	L2, U8
transmit	7	L4, U1
transport	6	L1, U1
trend	5	L1, U4
trigger	9	L4, U1
ultimate	**7**	**L3, U8**
undergo	10	L4, U9
underlie	6	L4, U5
undertake	4	L4, U2
uniform	7	L2, U4
unify	9	L2, U5
unique	**7**	**L3, U10**
utilize	**6**	**L3, U1**
valid	**3**	**L3, U8**
vary	1	L2, U1
vehicle	7	L1, U1
version	5	L1, U7
via	7	L4, U4
violate	9	L4, U3
virtual	**8**	**L3, U3**
visible	7	L2, U6
vision	9	L0, U8
visual	**8**	**L3, U7**
volume	3	L1, U8
voluntary	**7**	**L3, U10**
welfare	5	L4, U9
whereas	5	L4, U5
whereby	10	L4, U10
widespread	7	L2, U3

Oxford 3000™ words